VISUALIZATION FOR SUCCESS

VISUALIZATION
FOR SUCCESS

75
PSYCHOLOGICAL EMPOWERMENT
EXERCISES TO GET WHAT
YOU WANT IN LIFE

BARTON GOLDSMITH, PhD

ROCKRIDGE
PRESS

For general information on our other products and services or to obtain technical support, please contact our Customer Care Department within the United States at (866) 744-2665, or outside the United States at (510) 253-0500.

Rockridge Press publishes its books in a variety of electronic and print formats. Some content that appears in print may not be available in electronic books, and vice versa.

Interior and Cover Designer: Erik Jacobsen
Art Producer: Samantha Ulban
Editor: Mo Mozuch
Production Editor: Jenna Dutton
Cover Art © Shutterstock/MJgraphics
Author photo courtesy of © Angelika Goldsmith

ISBN: Print 978-1-64611-409-2 | eBook 978-1-64611-410-8
R0

*This book is dedicated to my lovely wife, Angelika.
I could never have visualized anyone as wonderful
as you coming into my life. You are what I live for,
and all my words are inspired by your love.*

Contents

Manifesting Your Goals

It's been a few years since a publisher asked me to write a book. I've had plenty to keep me busy with my writing and speaking, not to mention my on-set therapy practice. I'm not looking for more to do, but I like having a book in the pipeline. And not having one for a little while was kind of nibbling on my brain.

As we approach milestones in our lives, we consciously and unconsciously make changes to reach that goal. My blog for *Psychology Today* was approaching 20 million views, and I was proud of that number. But as I got closer to my goal, the views slowed down. It wasn't an illusion; other bloggers posted about "the drop" due to Google's new algorithms. It really didn't bother me—until it did. Even though I knew I would eventually get to 20 million, hitting that number became very important.

Somewhere in my unconscious mind, I not only equated reaching 20 million with my own satisfaction but was thinking that after I reached it, a book contract would magically pop out of my computer, and I would again be deep into another creative project. This motivated me to keep posting, and I did.

Once I hit the magic number, I received congratulatory emails, tons *more* views, and a sense of having done something helpful for my community of readers—but I still had no book contract. I began to wonder why. After all, I had good reason to expect a call. Most of my books had come out of the blue in this way, and one book had led to another, but having been off the charts for a bit, perhaps I'd fallen off the publishing radar? Still, I opened the computer every morning, thinking, "Well, maybe today."

For the next few weeks, I approached each day the same. Lots of things to write about. Lots of powerful energy going on around me. Waking, walking, and writing had become my focus. My wife was away, and I had to take care of our little dog who was recovering from an injury. We walk two or three times a day, and on those walks I imagined how I would rebalance my life when my other half returned, our dog-child was healed, and I had this new, imaginary project to complete.

Lo and behold, I was using a tool I had passionately studied, lectured, written about, and shared with many clients over many years. I was visualizing my goal of writing a new book. Generally, when I use visualization, it is directed and very conscious. But this time, I didn't think of my thoughts as having the same power. It proved to be a reminder of how strong our passing thoughts can be!

My blog was on fire, hitting 21 million after a million new views over two months, so I was feeling pretty good about my work. But not as good as I did when I got the email asking me to write a book on—get this—*Visualization for Success*! The amazing truth is that visualizing the book offer kept me going, and over time I was psychologically working toward my goal. That is how this book was born.

The lessons are clear: Our thoughts do create our reality, and we are almost always thinking. If you keep the thoughts positive, more good things happen. You can create a lot of what you want with intention and some internal visioning, and most of the time, it's easier than you think.

This book will teach you how to use the scientifically proven process of clinical visualization to help you achieve greater success in your life, your relationships, and your endeavors.

This book is not meant to serve as a substitute for professional counseling or medication, nor does it serve as an acknowledgment that the author has entered into a formal patient relationship with the reader. Anyone experiencing debilitating depression, anxiety, or other mental health ailments is encouraged to seek help from a licensed mental health professional.

PART I

THE FOUNDATION OF VISUALIZATION

Visualization has been around for thousands of years, mostly in spiritual and religious forms. In fact, prayer itself is a form of visualization. More recently, as chronicled in the classic *Getting Well Again*, researchers in the medical community began to study how visualization could help people with untreatable chronic or terminal illnesses. They examined how people could manage their pain and discomfort and feel more empowered just by doing exercises to visualize getting well. The effects were profoundly positive. Researchers and teachers like Dr. Milton Erickson helped refine the process and brought it to those who wish to enhance their overall performance in any area of life. A combination of these techniques is featured in this book and will focus on positivity, relationships, and goals.

CHAPTER 1

WHAT IS VISUALIZATION?

When Tiger Woods first won the Masters, everyone wanted to know more about his technique. How did he do it? He explained that before he took a swing, he would see the ball going into the hole. He visualized it. I have coached athletes, actors, and executives in the practice of visualization, and once they see how well it works, it becomes a major part of their personal game plan.

Visualization is a clinically proven cognitive practice for achieving success. It's simple and comfortable. It involves actively imagining and experiencing, with as many of your senses as possible, your desired outcomes in any area of your life.

A World of Positivity

The visualization process goes directly into your subconscious mind (where the vast majority of your actions are rooted) and gets you to a place of positivity by helping you concentrate on the things you want to achieve. As you visualize yourself reaching your goals, it creates a positive feeling that becomes wedded with those goals. Now any time you think about what you want to achieve, you feel good rather than uncomfortable or anxious. This positive unconscious response replaces negative thoughts that might accompany new or difficult circumstances and interfere with reaching your goals.

My colleague, college pal, and notable teacher of meditation and visualization, Dr. Sietze Vanderheide, JD, and I had a running joke through grad school. We bantered back and forth about an imaginary paper for some psychological journal on why the public picked blue as the new M&M color. Years later (and ago) I became the spokesperson for "My M&M's" (their personalized candies) and I thought of that conversation often. It's a sweet memory and another validation of how a casual and even playful imaginary goal is actually a visualization.

There are no mistakes in visualization. There are only better ways of finding what you want to feel and getting to where you want to go. The positive emotions from visualization spread from your mind to the rest of your body, and the motivation they create helps you focus on what is right for you rather than on fears of not getting it.

Creating Better Relationships

Visualization can also be used to improve your relationships. In fact, it is extremely powerful when both parties in a relationship, or all the members of a family or a team, visualize together, or as a group. Everyone gets to feel a more intense experience, which enhances the process, the productivity, and, ultimately, your relationships. Many people experience a serotonin rush during visualization. This brain chemical is very important for happiness and relaxation, so feelings of well-being are common.

In your primary relationship, visualization can be used to enhance intimacy, deepen communication, and resolve discord. Just doing a very simple visualization exercise together has saved many of my couple clients from useless arguments and negativity. It helped them feel the love they have for each other but have been unable to express. Doing this together boosts production of another brain chemical, oxytocin, also known as the "cuddle hormone." Couples in therapy who practice visualization on their own progress much faster.

Achieving Your Goals

We all have goals we want to achieve, and visualization is a tried-and-true way of helping reach them. Once you actually see something in your mind, it creates chemical changes that give you more self-confidence, thanks to the benefits of the reward hormone dopamine.

When you replace your negative thinking with positive visualization, you can immediately feel changes, both in your brain and in your body. This is an empowering experience. Doing it regularly will help you over-come self-limiting behaviors, those actions that block you from your goals. Our brains, bodies, and beings don't adjust quickly to serious emotional shifts. Visualization aids these psychological processes by helping you feel and see that you are making progress.

We know that visualization stimulates certain areas of the brain that control your ability to succeed. Scientists have studied the positive impact of mental imagery on brain regulation, showing new links between psychotherapy and neuroscience. In sports, we've seen that mental practice improves physical practice, and mental power can actually increase muscle power. For decades, the medical and psychological communities have used visualization to help patients cope with incurable and terminal illnesses. If visualization can help people with cancer, it can help you reach your desired goals.

History of Visualization

The practice of visualization goes back eons. It was used for spiritual and practical purposes by everyone from the Ancient Greeks to Native Americans. For example, sacred Native American dances before a buffalo hunt or a battle were actually very empowering group visualizations.

In the 1970s, Carl Simonton started getting positive results when he used the practice with cancer patients. David Bresler and Martin Rossman embraced these methods at the UCLA Pain Control Center. I was fortunate enough to study there with these two pioneers of the field.

Visualization was popularized by Shakti Gawain in her ground-breaking 1978 book *Creative Visualization*, which dramatically changed how we thought about and used the practice. It was no longer only for the chronically ill or for religious purposes. Now everyone could (and should) use it for whatever it is they would like to achieve.

Today this goal-setting practice is widely used in professional athletics, business, and education. And absolutely anyone can use it.

Visualization Process

The mind functions on a more effective level when you visualize. As you intensely focus on your goal, visualization creates neural pathways that reinforce a sense of eventual success. This process of neural imprinting is a powerful psychological tool because once imprinted, a thought or a goal more easily becomes a reality. For example, when an athlete sees herself winning a race, from start to finish, it becomes easier to win the actual race. Following visualization, your brain reads the goal as something you have already accomplished, which creates comfort, confidence, and a pathway to success.

Subconscious Vs. Conscious Mind

Consciousness is the state of awareness in internal or external existence. Basically, it's the fact that we know we are alive. Our conscious mind is what we use for daily functioning. Below our active thoughts lies the subconscious mind, which, according to Pierre Janet (1859–1947), who named it, is where powerful awareness can take place. Our subconscious mind is where most of our thoughts begin and where visualization has the biggest impact.

When using visualization, the inspiration and ideas go directly into our subconscious. The subconscious mind, in turn, feeds our conscious thoughts and controls most of our actions. This is how visualization increases your willpower and your cognitive ability to reach any goal.

Visualization works best when the mind is in a conscious but resting, or *alpha*, brainwave state. Alpha refers to the kind of brain waves you would experience when meditating or sitting quietly in a garden, a state of relaxation and openness.

Imagery

Imagery can best be described as the process of using the mind's eye as a means of seeing where you have been, where you are, and where you want to go. You direct your imagination to create just about anything you can think of, and you picture the steps to get there.

It's like LeBron James holding the ball at the free throw line, who pauses and imagines its arc toward the basket, to more easily make the shot. With mental imagery, brain functioning levels are increased many times over, and so is your ability. Knowing this and using it can help you achieve success.

Seeing the mental picture helps you advance the objective. As brain cells communicate, they get stronger and begin to multiply to meet the new task. Think of them as laying tracks for a bullet train that will help you reach your dreams of achievement.

Visual Perception

The process of visual perception begins with an object in the real world, just as the process of visualization begins with something in your imagination. Visual perception is a mental re-creation. Receptors in the eyes pick up the image of an object as a detailed pattern of neural activity, and the brain analyzes this information and transforms the neural signals to reveal what is there.

Similarly, when receptors in your brain are stimulated by imagery or a goal through visualization, they respond and transform the information as they anticipate absorbing all of what you are perceiving or hope to achieve. What you see in your mind's eye, real or imagined, is your perception. Visualization stimulates the brain, which sends and receives signals and interprets what is picked up as an image or a goal is formed in your mind.

The Four Stages of Visualization

Visualization can be broken down into a simple four-step process that allows you to use it effectively almost immediately. It is important to remember that this is a relaxing process, so don't stress out over it. Be patient and allow it to come to you.

Identify

Sometimes it can be difficult to identify exactly what it is you want or need to go after, but it's a critical first step. If you're having trouble, try a process of elimination: If you can identify everything that you don't want, logic dictates that what remains is what you do desire.

Visualization works best when you focus on a very specific goal. If there is something you'd like to have, or something you want to accomplish, and you are struggling to get there or feel like you need a little boost, visualization is the most available tool at your command.

Affirm

An affirmation is a positive phrase that gives you a focused shot of your mental projection or goals. An example is Émile Coué's famous affirmation, "Every day, in every way, I am getting better and better." An affirmation repeated throughout the day imprints on your brain, where it becomes part of your unconscious internal processing.

Affirmations are the seed of the visualization process. An affirmation will be used with each visualization exercise in this book. By repeating the affirmation, you are also repeating and strengthening your visualization. You can say it out loud or to yourself. Writing it down reinforces it at an even deeper subconscious level.

Picture

Mental imagery is perhaps the most important factor in a successful visualization process. Picturing your goal in your mind may initially seem simple, but the more detailed the image is, the more powerful your visualization will be.

For example, say your goal is to get your dream job. You need to visualize what and where that job would be, who else might be with you, how great your performance will be—you can even imagine a great review by your boss. Again, the more detailed, the stronger your visualization will become. Fill in as much of the picture in your mind as you can.

Release

The process of using your visualization is a bit like washing your hair: Shampoo, rinse, and repeat. The more you do your visualization

Getting the Full Picture:
Five Signs of Successful
Visualization

O bviously, if your goal is achieved immediately, like Tiger Woods getting a hole in one, you know the process is working. More likely, your goals are longer term, and reaching them will take a little more time.

Here are some signs that your visualization is working:

1. **The desire is always on your mind.** When you think about your goal, you do not feel stressed. You feel like that is where you belong.

2. **Your actions are becoming more aligned with your goal.** The details of your visualization are getting more precise.

3. **People are becoming part of the process.** As you move forward, you will have more interactions with people associated with your goal.

4. **Your ability to visualize will become stronger.** You will see it as a serious exercise that will help you achieve your goal.

5. **You are starting to see manifestations of your goal appear.** These may be in the form of offers, opportunities, or openings. Look for them.

If you see these signs, you'll know you are approaching your destination. Once you arrive, you'll need to adapt your visualization to reach the next level.

exercises, the better—but don't become obsessed. Practicing 10 to 30 minutes, one to three times a day, is plenty. It is not necessary to spend hours on the process; however, repeating your affirmations and remembering the picture throughout your day helps reinforce achievement of your goals.

There may be times when your stress level is so high that visualization becomes a way for you to rebalance and regain your peace of mind. Under those circumstances, longer visualizations can be helpful, as well as relaxation exercises such as deep yoga breathing or a progressive muscle relaxation (where you relax each part of your body starting top-down or from the bottom-up, relaxing your toes, then your feet, then ankles, and so on, moving up your body until you are completely relaxed). Visualization is always more effective when you incorporate all of your senses and emotions. The more you fully experience the visualization, the better it will work.

Essentials of Visualization Practice

Before you begin your visualization practice, you'll need to make sure you have all the essentials. Here are the four components to a successful visualization:

Timing Is Everything

Pick a time that works best for you and when you won't be disturbed. If possible, choose a time to regularly practice as part of your daily routine. Doing both morning and bedtime visualizations can really help the process. As mentioned earlier, you don't want to overdo it: 10 to 30 minutes, one to three times a day, is a good amount.

There will be situations when there is no good time, and you will have to visualize on the fly, so to speak. With some practice, doing a visualization while driving at 80 mph and running late to an appointment (the one you are currently visualizing!) may become second nature.

Find or Create a Good Space

It is best to be in a physical location that enhances the alpha state, which again is a relaxed but focused state of awareness. Being around water can help you relax and focus. Having a picture of water or water sounds in the background can also be calming.

Again, on occasion the space may not be ideal. The good news is that, with practice, visualization can make any discomfort more tolerable.

When You Are Blocked

Sometimes negative preconceptions about visualization can get in the way. Try to rid yourself of such thoughts as "This is silly," "I don't have a good imagination," or "I can't do this." Concentrate instead on your positive thoughts and your desired outcome.

You can also write down your positive thoughts and vision and then repeat these words to yourself during your visualization. You can even create a guided audio by recording what you've written. If you're still feeling blocked or just want some inspiration, guided audios are also available online, with background music and instructions on breathing, relaxation, and visualization. Guided audios can be soothing and particularly helpful during times of emotional crisis or high anxiety.

Another option is to get some coaching from a therapist who is trained in the practice of clinical guided imagery. This professional can even make a recording for you to use on your own (I have done this for many of my clients).

Relax Your Mind and Body to Fully
Relax Before You Start

Taking a few deep yoga breaths can be good, but doing a full-body relaxation and breathing process is even better.

You may want to try relaxing music, candles, or being outside in the fresh air—whatever will help you reach the desired state of mind. Make sure you're warm or cool enough and comfortably dressed. All these little things add up to making your experience a deep and transforming one.

Paint Your Perfect Picture

Dwell on the details: where you are, who you are with, what sights, sounds, tastes and smells reach your senses, what you are doing or saying. The more specific, the better. It is important to get emotionally involved with your visualization, so make sure that you are feeling good about what it is you are seeing in your mind's eye. Once you have the picture in your mind and you feel that your heart is in it, you are in the process of visualizing what you truly desire.

The Connection Between Psychology and Visualization

Psychology has always been at the root of visualization. For millennia, people have used visualization to help them get to where they want to go emotionally, spiritually, and professionally. It's simple navigation. Rather than trying to read a mental street map over and over, programming your goals into your subconscious GPS gets you there quicker and more easily.

Barriers, both emotional and practical, can get in the way, but with visualization you can bypass a lot of emotional processing and avoid the pitfalls of procrastination and self-doubt. This is because the process feeds your mind in a positive way and releases helpful brain chemicals like serotonin, dopamine, and oxytocin that further empower you to reach your goals.

Psychology's Role in Visualization

From a cognitive psychology perspective, healing and moving forward starts in your own mind. We know that people have the power to look at their situations from different perspectives. But how to get to a new perspective? One way is to visualize it. Visualization reaches into the subconscious levels of your brain to motivate you to focus on tasks you wish to accomplish. It is a form of cognitive therapy, where what you think affects your feelings and behavior.

Visualization also improves your mental attitude and outlook on life. Positive psychological messages from your visualizations counteract any self-limiting beliefs, thoughts of failure, or inappropriate behaviors that may be getting in the way.

Effectively, you are psyching yourself up for what it is that you want to accomplish. When the brain receives these positive images and messages, it gears up to take action. Your mind is able to bypass any negative past experiences that may have been causing a roadblock.

Therapeutic Applications

A therapeutic application is any process, exercise, or information that can be used to help people heal psychologically, emotionally, and even physically, and visualization is one of the best therapeutic applications out there. This positive, proactive, and practical tool can eliminate a great deal of stress and anxiety when you are faced with challenges, both new and old. Having a tried-and-true tool like this to advance your life is a real emotional boost and a huge time-saver.

In sports psychology, visualization is used to win, but it also helps athletes heal faster, build stronger teams, and create an environment of achievement. This seemingly complicated mental programming can all be done through the elegantly simple process of visualization.

For the rest of us, the therapeutic applications work in a similar way. The most valuable applications are positivity, relationships, and goals—that is, the focus of this book. By using visualization to change your mood or your energy from negative to positive, you can return to your creative and intellectual baseline and move forward.

How to Picture/See Your Visualization

There are three different methods for visualization. You can use whichever method you like, or try all three.

1. **You are watching a movie and you are the main character.** Watch yourself doing what it is that you wish to accomplish as if you were at the movies or watching television (it can even be a cartoon).

2. **You are in your own movie.** This is not about being the star; it's about living the part and feeling the energy around you as you move forward and watch yourself reaching your goals. You can also think of this as a first-person visualization.

3. **You are the movie director.** This is where you direct the process and the players. You are moving things and people with your mind and imagination as you watch yourself achieve the desired result.

These methods are really about your sense of perspective. You may want to start with whichever feels most natural.

Key Concepts and Tips for Successful Visualization

The following are some common terms and phrases that will come up in the visualization instructions in Part II, along with tips for how to get the most out of these exercises.

ALPHA STATE OR ALPHA BRAIN WAVE STATE: The easiest way to understand the alpha state is to compare it with how you feel when you go to a relaxing movie or concert. As you get into the alpha state, you are seeing and hearing what's going on in front of you and are oblivious to the outside world. The essence of this mental state is being calm and tuned in at the same time. The exercises ahead will ask you to "get into the alpha state," which means just relaxing and allowing yourself to focus on the images in your mind.

COGNITIVE ABILITIES: Your cognitive abilities are your rational thinking, learning, and problem-solving skills. Visualization is a cognitive skill set, as it requires all three of these mental processes.

CONSCIOUSNESS: A state of awareness in internal or external existence. Bringing something into consciousness doesn't mean just being awake. It means thinking about whatever you want to bring to mind and being aware of your feelings at the same time.

MENTAL VS. EMOTIONAL: Mental is what's in your head, how you think about something or imagine it in your mind; emotional is what's in your heart.

MINDFULNESS: A form of meditation in which you concentrate on being in the present moment, noticing everything in that moment without judging anything. By practicing visualization, you are practicing a form of mindfulness.

MIND'S EYE: The mind's eye is your movie screen for your imagination or focus. This is where your ideas and thoughts are seen by your brain, evaluated by your mind, and felt by your heart. It is also where you can make changes to your thoughts and goals, as well as accept where you are and plan where you want to go.

NOTICE: This mindfulness technique means that you observe something without involving your emotions or judgment. In visualizations, you use this technique to keep triggers or negative thoughts from interrupting the positive imagery.

PROGRESSIVE MUSCLE RELAXATION: A good way to begin any visualization or whenever you want to release tension. Best done lying down or comfortably seated, close your eyes and gradually relax your body, noticing and relaxing every muscle, from your head down to your toes, or vice versa.

PSYCHE: The entire thinking process, unconscious, subconscious, and conscious. Simply put—your whole mind.

RELAXATION BREATHING (ALSO DEEP YOGA BREATHING OR RELAXED DEEP BREATHING): Inhale very slowly through your nose, filling your entire chest; hold your breath for several seconds; and then slowly exhale through your mouth. Repeat three times to fully relax.

TRIGGER: An action, thought, or words (either spoken to you or repeated inside your mind) that cause you feelings of high stress and discomfort. Feeling triggered is a strong emotional and physical response, making you want to fight back or flee a situation. In visualizations, you can notice your triggers without getting caught up in them.

SUBCONSCIOUS: The part of the mind which is inaccessible to the conscious mind but which affects behavior and emotions.

PART II

VISUALIZE SUCCESS

This part of the book will take you through a number of practical visualization exercises, as you focus on the three main components of success: positivity, relationships, and goals. Each of these areas corresponds to particular parts and activities of the brain. Positivity is located in the prefrontal cortex (PFC) of the brain, and thinking positively makes your brain more flexible. This is because of neuroplasticity, or the ability of the brain to change continuously through your life. Goal-setting also begins in the PFC, and enhances the production of dopamine and serotonin. Our relationships and emotions are controlled by the amygdala, and in good relationships, you build the cuddle hormone, oxytocin.

By stimulating these areas, visualization improves brain functioning and your ability to succeed. Visualization will help you reach your dreams in a new and life-enhancing way.

CHAPTER 2

POSITIVITY

We all know it's pretty hard to do anything if you feel negative about it. And even if you do get the job done, there's no joy in it if you feel your skills and efforts are being wasted or exploited.

Positive visualizations can change how you view the world. If seeing things in a good light has been challenging lately or even throughout your life, doing these exercises will give you the power to change your outlook.

With this newfound positivity, you will have more energy and experience more joy, and your creativity will be alive and flowing. Having a positive attitude about life is like taking off a blindfold. You will see things with greater clarity.

Case Study

One of my favorite positive success stories is that of Sir Richard Branson, the founder of Virgin Group. Virgin Group is now a multinational venture capital conglomerate, but Branson started with one record store in London before he began recording musicians and selling their records for less than the competition. It was a tremendous success. He eventually signed the Rolling Stones, bought an airline, a railroad, and is now flying into outer space.

It wasn't always an upward trajectory. When someone asked Branson how to become a millionaire, he quipped, "Be a billionaire and buy an airline." He may have had a few difficult moments, but he has never lost his positive attitude. Those early losses are probably just pocket change compared to what he has today.

He is a champion of positive thinking and has used it to the benefit of many, many people. Positive thinking is a major part of his business and personal belief system. One of my favorite SRB quotes is: "If somebody offers you an amazing opportunity, but you are not sure you can do it, say yes—then learn how to do it later!" And in my mind, the best way to do that is through positive visualization. Simply see yourself doing what you want and doing it well. That will bring you what you desire in life.

Positive thinking has been around for a long time, first popularized in 1952 by Norman Vincent Peale's book *The Power of Positive Thinking*. It's still a bestseller, and why? Because it works. Using the concept of positivity and amplifying it with visualization is a bit like moving from an acoustic guitar to an electric one plugged into an array of amps—it's simply more powerful.

If we don't take risks, we don't grow very much. It is by trying new things that we make our dreams come true, and the whole process is more successful and feels much better when we do it with a positive attitude.

Guidelines for Cultivating Positivity

You cultivate positivity with positive thoughts. But how can you tell the difference between positive thoughts and self-limiting or negative thoughts? The easiest way is to check in with how you feel emotionally and physically. If anxiety is connected with a thought, it might not be the right one for you (even if the thought excites you). Positive thoughts make you feel good in your mind and body. These are the thoughts you want to cultivate.

POSITIVITY EXERCISE 1
GETTING TO POSITIVE

Positive thoughts emanate from positive actions, like this visualization. The goal here is to open your mind to new positive actions and feelings that might be available. Cognitive psychology tells us that the direct approach is best, so in this visualization, allow your mind to go where it wants to go at first. Evaluate where you are and then make a decision where to move forward. If this feels familiar, it's because this is how we process many of our decisions, and if we can keep things in a positive place, that processing becomes very easy. This is also a good group exercise.

Time:	15–30 minutes
Place:	This exercise can be done indoors or out, at any time of day that is comfortable for you.
Level:	Beginner
Affirmation:	I am allowing positive thoughts and feelings to enter my life.

Steps:

1. Begin with your relaxation breathing, and allow your mind to relax as well. Your eyes should be closed so that your heart is fully engaged. Enter the alpha state.

2. Remember the last time you felt really positive about something, and spend a little time in that place. Where were you? Who were you with? What was the time of day? What were the circumstances? Sense the feeling of positivity that accompanies this memory throughout your body, brain, and being.

3. Now, look at your current life and take the feeling from your positive recent memory and let it wash over you. Visualize doing this in any way that works for you: You could imagine sinking into a warm bath or wrapping up in a warm towel. The idea is to blend in those positive feelings, so you feel them now and when you open your eyes. That way they will stay with you for a while.

POSITIVITY EXERCISE 2
APPRECIATING MY SURROUNDINGS

Everyone wants to feel appreciated. The best way to have it come to you is to be able to feel it for yourself and your life right now as well as what your life will be. If you spend only 10 minutes a day in appreciation of where you are and what you have, it will make you feel good. This positive action sends messages to your brain and body that will lift your spirits and give you more energy.

Time:	10–15 minutes
Place:	Comfortably seated, indoors or out. This exercise can also be done while walking.
Level:	Beginner
Affirmation:	My life is a beautiful place to be.

Steps:

1. Find a comfortable position. You can be seated or lying down, indoors or out. This exercise can also be done while you are standing or walking.

2. Begin with your relaxation breathing, and enter the alpha state. If you have closed your eyes, imagine yourself in your favorite personal place. It can be someplace you know, like a favorite chair in your home, or a peaceful place you create, like the seashore on a summer's day.

3. Look at only the good in your life right now. Find what you have that you can (or should) appreciate. Look at your health and see the positives, your home, and the people you know and love. Now use all of your senses to appreciate your imaginary surroundings and make them part of you. Use your ears and listen for answers in your imaginary surroundings—the cozy fire in the hearth crackling or the ocean waves crashing. If there are smells in the air, take those in, too, as well as any tastes you might have, such as the saltiness of the ocean breeze. And, most important, physically and emotionally feel your experience. If you are seated in a comfortable chair, imagine the comfort of the cushions under you and the contentment in your heart.

4. Bring that appreciation into your consciousness and allow it to continue to move through your body so that you can really feel it in the here and now.

POSITIVITY EXERCISE 3
LETTING GO OF THE PAST

Are there some negative things in your past that you feel hold you back or that you just can't let go of? The mind can hold on to uncomfortable thoughts and experiences for a long time. This visualization will help you move forward. Letting those thoughts and memories go is just a matter of patience and practice. When you do, you will feel so much lighter, and you can continue this practice to keep you from building up other negativity.

Time:	10–15 minutes
Place:	Comfortably seated, indoors or out
Level:	Beginner
Affirmation:	My past does not control my present or my future.

Steps:

1. Find a comfortable position. You can be seated or lying down, indoors or out.

2. Begin with your relaxation breathing to enter the alpha state. Imagine yourself in peaceful surroundings. It can be someplace you know or a peaceful place you create.

3. Begin with the appreciation exercise in Positivity Exercise 2 (page 26). See your life as it is in this moment. Look for the good. If negative thoughts or memories pop in, imagine you are erasing them like they were on a white board, and watch them disappear. Or imagine you are sitting by the edge of a stream, placing the negative thoughts or memories into the water and letting them drift away. Let them go. Concentrate on the feeling of release. How do you feel now?

4. Bring that emotion into your consciousness and allow it to move through your body. Experience it with all of your senses so that you can really feel it in the present.

POSITIVITY EXERCISE 4
THE WALKING VISUALIZATION

Having negative thoughts and feelings affects our entire thinking and performance process. By combining a little light exercise with the process of visualization, you can bring in more positive thoughts.

Time:	10–15 minutes
Place:	Outside, while walking
Level:	Beginner
Affirmation:	I am bringing new and positive things into my world.

Steps:

1. Get ready to go for a walk. If you have dogs, you can take them along. This is a walking exercise, but it can also be done seated by a big window with a view if you cannot go outside.

2. Begin with your relaxation breathing, best done before you leave the house. Focus on entering the alpha state.

3. Now go outside. You can be outside your office or your home or anywhere. It doesn't matter. The goal is to find 20 new things on this walk (and each time you do this exercise). For example, you may notice new trees and flowers or architecture. You may also notice the air and the wind and how it makes you feel. Does it lighten you up or make you want to hide from it? If you do your walking at night, you can look at the stars and imagine what it's like to be a tourist in outer space.

4. Notice how it feels to find new things to see and appreciate, and how it feels to have accomplished this goal while walking.

5. Now picture yourself achieving your current goal(s) in life. Allow yourself to feel that successful feeling. As you watch and feel yourself succeed at your goal, notice that you now believe you will reach it. Keep that feeling going for the rest of your walk.

6. If you like, write down some of the new things you remember seeing from your walk (you don't have to remember them all). The ones you do recall will have deeper meaning for you.

POSITIVITY EXERCISE 5
BRINGING IN THE LIGHT

Most of us have moments, and sometimes days, when we are plagued by uncomfortable thoughts. Fortunately, there is a way to remove them. You can simply replace uncomfortable or negative needs with comfortable or positive thoughts and images. What you see in your visualization will be a transition from negative thinking to positive thinking.

Time:	10–15 minutes
Place:	Seated comfortably, indoors or out
Level:	Beginner
Affirmation:	I am letting go of my uncomfortable thoughts.

Steps:

1. Find a comfortable position. Begin with your relaxation breathing, and allow your mind to relax as well as you enter the alpha state.

2. Find an area of discomfort in your life and bring it to mind or consciousness. It could be a problem at work or with someone you know or anything that is bothering you. As you bring this problem to mind, notice how you feel. Do not hold on to this feeling, just notice it.

3. Next, visualize a white healing light all around you. Feel the warmth of the light gently bathing you and your discomfort, making it dissolve. As you continue to bathe in the light, visualize your discomfort dissolving and lifting away from you.

4. Allow this process to continue for as long as it feels good. What you experience in this exercise can help you later if something is troubling you. Just close your eyes and remember the image of the light and feel its calming comfort. You can wrap your troubles in the light and release those negative thoughts.

POSITIVITY EXERCISE 6
FINDING AND KEEPING MY BALANCE

Keeping your life balanced adds to the positivity you experience. This means making sure that you don't let one part of your life (whether it's relationships, work, or something else) dominate all your time and energy. Being out of balance opens the door to stress, anger, and discomfort (inside and out). We strive to get things done but forget to keep our life in balance—and this does not mean going from one extreme to another! True balance lies somewhere in the middle, and being there minimizes stress and enhances your ability to feel the joy of life.

Time:	10–15 minutes
Place:	Seated comfortably, indoors or out
Level:	Beginner/Intermediate
Affirmation:	My life is continuously staying in balance.

Steps:

1. Get comfortable. Begin with your relaxation breathing and allow your mind to relax. Enter the alpha state.

2. Allow yourself to see one area of your life that you feel is out of balance, and then physically feel and visualize what it is like for you to deal with this. Are you feeling stressed? What do you need to do to find balance? Picture a more balanced life.

3. Now imagine an old-fashioned apothecary scale, maybe made of brass, with a plate suspended on either side of its central post. Imagine one of the plates is weighted down with all your concerns or priorities, so it is lower than the other plate, which sits empty. Now imagine taking small stones or weights and adding them, one by one, to the other plate. These stones or weights represent other things in your life that you've been neglecting; they could be your relationships, your health, your work, whatever it is that you have been ignoring as your life has been out of balance. What happens as you add the stones to the plate that you've been neglecting?

4. Watch as this plate gathers weight and the other plate lifts to meet it halfway, so that the parts of your life are now in balance.

POSITIVITY EXERCISE 7
SMELLING THE ROSES

We all need to take a little more time to stop and smell the roses. We also need to learn how to grow and nurture this feeling of joy in ourselves. The process may take a little while to take hold, but if you continue this exercise in available moments, it will increase the joy in your life and free your mind from its worries and woes. Finding a little joy in life helps you realize that you may have been hard on yourself—and you're right, of course. Doing this exercise will help you regain your peace of mind.

Time:	10–15 minutes
Place:	Outdoors, in a flower garden
Level:	Beginner/Intermediate
Affirmation:	I will remember to stop and smell the roses.

Steps:

1. Find a garden with roses or flowers growing at a time of year when they are in bloom.

2. Do your relaxation breathing to enter the alpha state, and then take a walk among the flowers.

3. When you walk by a rose bush in bloom, stop and notice every-thing. Notice the beauty of the flowers, the shapes, the colors, the light playing on the leaves. Allow yourself to appreciate this visual presentation of life. Plant the picture of the rose in your mind.

4. Now smell the roses. Breathe in deeply and make it a memory. Inhale the sweet scent with your eyes open, and again with your eyes closed so that your brain, body, and senses are fully engaged in the experience.

POSITIVITY EXERCISE 8
FINDING HAPPINESS WITHIN

Happiness is not a destination. It is someplace already inside you, but sometimes it is hard to see and feel. This visualization will teach you how to draw on what is already available within your own mind and heart. Happiness is never constant—no one gets to be happy all the time—but it is a place we get to visit and enjoy. And don't be hard on yourself for just feeling content, as that's really a great place to be, too. Spending time in that headspace is very healthy.

Time:	10–15 minutes
Place:	Indoors or outside
Level:	Beginner/Intermediate
Affirmation:	I am a happy person.

Steps:

1. Get comfortable, and begin with your relaxation breathing. As you relax, put your hands over your heart. Focus on entering the alpha state.

2. Begin to recall a happy moment. Concentrate on a particular memory, perhaps from your childhood, that fun birthday when your mom and dad hired the magician. Or it could be a more recent memory of traveling to a beautiful island or of going someplace closer to home while camping with good friends. Any happy memory is appropriate. Picture the details of the moment, your surroundings, who was there, the sights, smells, the laughter, the feeling of the air.

3. As you relive the happy moment, take in the feeling and dwell on it. Does it make you smile? Concentrate on each part of your body, the feeling of happiness and calm as it washes over you.

4. Continue to concentrate on this feeling as long as you can, as it becomes a new memory. Once you have imprinted any emotion, you can recall it whenever you need to. That is one of the many gifts of visualization.

POSITIVITY EXERCISE 9
BUILDING SELF-CONFIDENCE

It is hard to feel positive when you do not feel confident: A lack of confidence can prevent you from feeling good about being alive or about what you are doing. But the opposite is also true; when you are feeling confident, you love life and feel that you can do most anything that you might want to do. You can make things happen around you, but more importantly, confidence helps you feel good about yourself. When you feel confident, life is just better.

Time:	10–15 minutes
Place:	Indoors or outside, in a comfortable spot
Level:	Beginner/Intermediate
Affirmation:	I am a very confident person.

Steps:

1. Choose a time of day that is comfortable for you. If possible, do it in the morning to get a good start on the day. Begin with your relaxation breathing, and allow your mind to relax. Now close your eyes and enter the alpha state.

2. Remember a time in your life when you were feeling very confident. Try to focus on a particular moment when you felt great. Perhaps it was a moment when you accomplished something that you'd been working really hard on. It could be when you received an award or acknowledgment of some kind. You may have won an athletic event or gotten a promotion. Or you may have simply received a smile from someone you think you really might like.

3. Remember as much as you can about the moment, your surroundings, who was there with you, and remember how you felt. Let that feeling of confidence sit within you for a few minutes, so you really appreciate all the sensations—physical, emotional, and mental.

4. Imagine that feeling of confidence flowing into your current body and being. Let it sit inside you for several minutes.

POSITIVITY EXERCISE 10
BEING GRATEFUL FOR MY LIFE

Gratitude is one of the most powerful emotions you can feel. Gratitude has a deep psychological effect that is profoundly motivational. Gratitude can not only change the way you look at life but actually bring more of what you want into your world. When feeling low, it's sometimes hard to remember to be thankful for all that has come to you, so it's important to stop to appreciate your life, those you love, and all that you have created. This visualization is good to do on your own or as part of a group. This is a great couple, family, or team visualization.

Time:	15–30 minutes
Place:	Indoors or outside, at any time of day
Level:	Beginner/Intermediate
Affirmation:	I am grateful for all the good that has come into my life, and there is room for more.

Steps:

1. Begin with your relaxation breathing, and allow your mind to relax as well. Your eyes can be open or closed. Focus on entering the alpha state.

2. Look at your life and begin counting your blessings (hopefully this will take a while). Imagine thanking each person who has helped you along the way to becoming who you are today and for what you have. You can also thank any higher power you may feel connected to. See as many of the events and people you are grateful for as you can and allow yourself to emotionally and physically feel your gratitude. (Note: The next time you come back to this visualization, do your best to see other people who have helped you get to where you are.)

3. Now also take a moment to acknowledge and thank yourself for doing the hard work that got you here.

4. See all this gratitude moving through your body, and imagine it making you stronger in many ways. Focus on each part of your body, from your head down to your toes, feeling relaxed, calmed, grateful. This added dimension is very empowering.

POSITIVITY EXERCISE 11
MENTAL EMPOWERMENT

Mentally strong people have an advantage. They are able to overcome setbacks more rapidly and tend to be better problem solvers. Mental strength is not about being smarter but about being more cognitively aware. Mental strength helps you see problems before they happen and helps you solve the ones currently on your plate. This mental empowerment visualization will help you build confidence in your own mental strength. It will also help you with decision making. You can do this visualization on your own or as part of a group.

Time:	10–20 minutes
Place:	Indoors or outside, at a time of day that is comfortable for you
Level:	Beginner/Intermediate
Affirmation:	I am mentally strong and powerful.

Steps:

1. Begin with your relaxation breathing, and allow your mind to relax as well. Your eyes should be closed as you enter the alpha state.

2. See yourself searching for an answer to a question. The question may be real—such as "Should I ask for a raise?"—or imaginary. It doesn't matter. Just picture yourself searching with a question.

3. Now imagine yourself going to a place to look for the answer to your question. It can be in a room where you find a page with a secret code for only your eyes to see, or it could be in a special file in your computer-like brain. You have the tools to find your answer. See yourself getting the answer and feeling confident in your mental strength.

4. Feel your mind getting stronger. Visualize it and know that you are able to complete the tasks that are before you.

POSITIVITY EXERCISE 12
MAKING TIME TO PLAY

When things are getting intense in your work life, it's important to make time to play. No matter what your hobby is or what activities you love doing, they are all positive. The hardest part may be putting work aside for a few hours so you can enjoy life.

If you do not have some outlet to express your joy, you can lose your drive; your psyche gets too exhausted. Know that life requires balance, and play is a part of that. Look within and see what it is that you would love to be doing. Travel, sports, games, playing music, and gardening, to name a few, are all healthy play.

Time:	10–15 minutes
Place:	Indoors or outside, at any time of day that is comfortable for you
Level:	Beginner/Intermediate
Affirmation:	I enjoy play and give myself the time to enjoy it.

Steps:

1. Begin with your relaxation breathing, and allow your mind to relax and enter the alpha state. Your eyes should be closed so that your imagination is doing all the work.

2. See yourself engaged and enjoying one of your favorite activities. Allow yourself to feel the joy that you get from this "play," and bring that feeling into your mind and body.

3. As you feel the joy from playing, ask yourself what other activities you might enjoy or have always wanted to do. Come up with some new ideas for fun outlets to pursue.

4. Feel your body getting relaxed, exercised, and joyful, so your mind is inspired to hold on to those feelings, bringing you the energy to play more.

POSITIVITY EXERCISE 13
FROM NEGATIVE TO NEUTRAL

We all have negative moments in our lives: a scary email or message, a feeling of not being able to complete a project, or a misunderstanding with someone important in our lives. Such negative interactions can throw you off your game. This visualization will help you move from a negative to a more neutral outlook, which is a step toward positive. For most people, the psychological leap straight from negative to positive is an intimidating task, which is why we go to neutral first. Note: This can also be a great group exercise.

Time:	15–30 minutes
Place:	Indoors or outside, at a time of day that is comfortable for you
Level:	Beginner/Intermediate
Affirmation:	I no longer hold on to negativity.

Steps:

1. Begin with your relaxation breathing, and allow your mind to relax. Your eyes should be closed so that your heart is fully engaged. Enter the alpha state.

2. Locate where the feeling of negativity is in your body. It could be your chest or somewhere else. Keep looking until you find it, and then place your hand over the spot.

3. Focus all of your attention on this place in your body. Dwell on the feeling of your hand over this spot, how it warms and comforts you. If your mind wanders, bring your attention back to the place where your hand is.

4. Keep your attention on the feeling of your hand over this spot and your body, and you will begin to notice your emotion getting lighter and lighter, until it finally disappears.

POSITIVITY EXERCISE 14
THE PERFECT VACATION

Most people take vacations in order to relax and feel more positive, and it usually works . . . until you get back home. By using the power of positive visualization, you can keep the vacation going (and even make some practical choices that will make your next trip away even nicer). This exercise relies on your memory, and each time you do it, you will remember new things. This helps you take in the positive experience so it stays with you until your next adventure. Our memory can serve us in many ways, and providing emotional comfort is a great use of the mind.

Time:	10–15 minutes
Place:	Indoors or outside, at a time of day that is comfortable for you
Level:	Intermediate/Advanced
Affirmation:	My holidays and vacations are memorable and make my life lighter.

Steps:

1. Begin with your relaxation breathing, and allow your mind to relax as you enter the alpha state.

2. The first time you do this exercise, allow the memories of your favorite vacations to come up on their own. As you recall them, put an imaginary star by the ones that are the most special (so you can come back to them later).

3. Choose one of the memories and concentrate your focus on the memory of that vacation. Bring it to mind, so you can visualize some favorite aspects. Feel where you are, smell the air, hear the waves or the wind, touch the sand or the earth or water. Use as many of your senses as possible to take in and deeply memorize the feeling of this place.

4. Once you have established that this is your favorite place, you can come back to the present whenever you like. (Many people use these memories for future visualizations when they want to imagine going somewhere peaceful.)

POSITIVITY EXERCISE 15
CONSOLIDATING THE GAINS

Asking a client "What have you learned?" is a tried-and-true methodology for therapists, typically used at the end of a session. It's known as *consolidating the gains*, and the principle is also a great tool for visualization. Seeing your growth since you have begun this practice will positively reinforce how far you have come, which, in turn, is both validating and motivating for your psyche and will inspire you to continue moving forward.

Time:	10–20 minutes
Place:	Indoors or outside, at a time of day that is comfortable for you
Level:	Intermediate
Affirmation:	I have grown and continue to grow through the practice of positive visualization.

Steps:

1. Begin with your relaxation breathing, and allow your mind to relax. Your eyes should be closed. Be seated with your back straight. Focus on entering the alpha state.

2. Remember why you bought this book. Recall your motivation and the things you wanted to accomplish with visualization.

3. Now look at how you are doing now. Recognize how you have already grown and learned new tools to help you feel more positive. Are you able to bring more into your life? Are you feeling better than you did when you started the practice? Allow positive feelings to wash over you in this moment of recognition.

4. Invite yourself to see how you will be growing in the future. See yourself doing better and better each time you do an exercise or face a new challenge. As you visualize your progress, feel the success of accomplishment.

POSITIVITY EXERCISE 16
FROM SADNESS TO CONTENTMENT

Just as it is unreasonable to think that you can immediately go from negative to positive without first shifting into neutral, going from sad to happy takes an intermediate step: finding contentment. Sadness holds you back from being able to feel simply okay. In fact, contentment with life is a deeper and longer lasting feeling than happiness, which comes and goes. Pushing yourself to be happy is exhausting and fruitless, but allowing yourself to be in a state of contentment is fairly easy and a great gift.

Time:	10–20 minutes
Place:	Indoors or outside, at a time of day that is comfortable for you. Be seated with your back straight.
Level:	Intermediate
Affirmation:	I feel content with myself and the life I live.

Steps:

1. Begin with your relaxation breathing, and allow your mind to relax. Your eyes should be closed as you feel yourself enter the alpha state.

2. Picture the sadness you are currently feeling, but don't allow yourself to wallow. Step back and observe from a neutral place. Visualize the circumstances, as if you were watching from a distance (as if seeing yourself in a movie). You do not need to feel the negative emotions.

3. Now allow yourself to take an objective look at your entire life, and recall a moment of contentment, when you were feeling good—not elated, but actually okay about the way things were going. Think of a specific moment. Perhaps it was as you were reading a favorite book, or perhaps it was a feeling you had after a conversation. Something simple. Recall your surroundings, whether you were by yourself or with others, and remember the feeling of contentment you felt in that moment.

4. Now layer that feeling of contentment over your sadness (you might be able to imagine it as a light mist) and feel that contentment in your mind and body.

POSITIVITY EXERCISE 17
FROM CONTENTMENT TO JOY

Now that you have experienced contentment, your psyche is ready to take in some joy. Feeling emotions of joy creates tremendous inspiration. Joy is perhaps our greatest motivator. Use it to help you get to the next level, but be aware that it is not a constant in your universe, which is fine. If you learn to default to contentment, the joyful moments will be more available to you.

Time:	10–15 minutes
Place:	Indoors or outside, at a time of day that is comfortable for you. Be seated with your back straight.
Level:	Intermediate
Affirmation:	I am bringing in and feeling more joy in my life every day.

Steps:

1. Begin with your relaxation breathing, and allow your mind to relax and enter the alpha state. Your eyes can be open or closed.

2. Create a picture in your mind's eye of what joy looks like to you. It's okay to use past experiences or create imaginary new ones. Perhaps you will think of the moment you found out you would be a new parent, or when you realized you were in love, or the moment you hit that ball out of the park.

3. Whatever you remember or imagine, recall the feeling you had, and let it spread over you. The important thing is to see it and feel it. This process imprints the feeling of joy within you and makes it a part of you.

4. See yourself feeling joyful, and just stay with the picture and the feeling moving through your brain and body.

POSITIVITY EXERCISE 18
OVERCOMING FEAR

Fear is one of the things that holds us back. By lessening and eliminating the fear factor, almost anything is possible. Most rational fear comes from having had a bad experience, and irrational fear can come from avoiding experiences we've never had. With visualization, that can be changed. As you visualize yourself doing or saying something that frightens you (such as giving a speech in public), your mind and body will become familiar with the experience in your subconscious. The first time you actually try what you thought about will be only mildly frightening (if that), and you will do it better than you ever thought you could.

Time:	10–15 minutes
Place:	Indoors or outside, at a time of day that is comfortable for you. Be seated with your back straight.
Level:	Intermediate
Affirmation:	I am not afraid of the tasks and people I face in my life.

Steps:

1. Begin with your relaxation breathing, and allow your mind to relax and enter the alpha state. Your eyes can be open or closed.

2. Once you have fully relaxed, look inside and see what it is that is frightening you right now. It could be a situation, it could be a person you don't want to see, or it could be a difficult task at work—whatever you have been avoiding.

3. Now imagine yourself approaching the thing that you fear—this situation, person, or task. Imagine the steps you would take, what you would do or bravely say. See yourself doing what you need to do, and see that you are doing an outstanding job. (Alternatively, you could imagine this fear as being drawn on a whiteboard that you erase.)

4. Feel the success of having overcome your fears to succeed at something you have never tried before. Feel the pride in what you have accomplished.

POSITIVITY EXERCISE 19
THE PERFECT DAY

Many of us are hard on ourselves because we are not perfect, and it is a waste of valuable human energy. Trying to be perfect is all too common, but it can hold us back from enjoying life because, in truth, very little is perfect. That being said, who you are is perfect, and so are your imperfections. Accepting yourself for being a flawed human being (like the rest of us) will help you feel more positive about your life. All that time and energy that you've been wasting on trying to be perfect can now be put to better use.

Time:	10–15 minutes
Place:	Indoors or outside, at a time of day that is comfortable for you. Be seated with your back straight.
Level:	Intermediate
Affirmation:	I am perfectly imperfect.

Steps:

1. Begin with your relaxation breathing, and allow your mind to relax and enter the alpha state. Your eyes should be closed.

2. Recall a time when you made a mistake and were hard on yourself. It may help to look from a distance, as if you were watching it happen from the outside. It may have been something you said to someone, or something you did that you later regretted. Recall what happened and the way you felt about yourself later. Note but try not to dwell on the feelings. It might help to think of yourself watching what happened as if you were a friend, looking back from the present. Now forgive yourself, the same way you would forgive a friend. Say to yourself, "It's okay. No one is perfect."

3. If you can't remember a recent time, then see yourself in the past, as a child or even as an infant. At that stage, we are all perfect.

4. As you visualize, see and feel that your imperfections, mistakes, and flaws do not take away from your essence as a perfect being. In fact, they make you more human and accepting.

POSITIVITY EXERCISE 20
I AM GOOD ENOUGH

Feeling that you are not good enough is one of the biggest blocks to having positive feelings. Your brain is getting mixed signals, and when it senses self-doubt, it tends to shut itself down. To prevent that, you must refill those parts of the brain with self-esteem. No matter where life has taken you, if you want to move forward emotionally, you have to accept that you have what it takes to get to the next level. This also reflects on your practical life as well. What you feel within is always projected out and picked up on by others. If you feel that you are more than good enough, that is the first thing others will sense.

Time:	10–15 minutes
Place:	Indoors or outside, at a time of day that is comfortable for you. Be seated with your back straight.
Level:	Intermediate
Affirmation:	I am good enough.

Steps:

1. Relax and breathe deeply. Enter the alpha state. Now close your eyes.

2. Find that part of yourself that feels that you aren't good enough and visualize what that looks like. Visualize yourself from a little distance away, so you are seeing yourself in this moment or as you were when you were younger. Come up with a specific moment of when you felt not good enough, such as when someone else was chosen for the school team. You must look for, find, and connect with that "not enough" part of yourself.

3. Now imagine yourself as a friend in that moment, and tell yourself that you are good enough. That event does not define you. Now bring that feeling into the present. With each breath and each feeling of not-enoughness in the moment, allow the friend voice inside you to remind you that you are good enough.

4. You might find this a little awkward at first, but stay with the process until you are able to trust this new voice and feel its reassurance in your mind and body. This visualization works best if you repeat it every day for a week.

POSITIVITY EXERCISE 21
ATTITUDE ADJUSTMENT

In some short-term situations, it's important to be able to quickly shift from negative to positive, jumping right over neutral. When you are heading somewhere you don't want to go or when you have to deal with difficult people, you can just make a decision to not get triggered and to have a good time. This decision can work wonders. The psychological and practical benefit is that you will enjoy yourself and avoid feeling negative about something you can't really control. It's a choice, and all starts in your brain.

Time:	10–15 minutes
Place:	Indoors or outside, or on the go
Level:	Intermediate
Affirmation:	I am going to enjoy this experience.

Steps:

1. Try this as you are walking into someplace you don't particularly like, or have to talk with people you'd rather avoid. It can also be done after parking the car (before you enter the building).

2. Breathe and relax. Keep your eyes and your heart open. (This can also be done as a seated, closed-eye visualization if you have time.)

3. See yourself enjoying (or not hating) the experience of going inside.

4. Imagine encountering someone you don't really care for, and imagine them in a glass dome from where they can't impact you. (Or you can put an imaginary glass dome over yourself to shield you from people who rub you the wrong way.)

5. When you're ready, end the visualization and go inside. Remember to smile as you go in. Knowing that you have the ability to protect yourself and change your mood is empowering, and using it when you need to is powerfully positive. Know that and take it in as part of this process.

POSITIVITY EXERCISE 22
SEEING THE GOOD

If you aren't a naturally positive person, it is possible to become one. But you have to do the work. The good news is that you can make the choice. When you first start out, you may have to practice daily, visualizing yourself feeling positive, and that effort will eventually stick. If your psyche tends to lean toward the negative, it could be biochemical, heredity, or just habit, but in all those cases you can change it. By using visualization, you can reverse negative thinking patterns.

Time:	10–15 minutes
Place:	Indoors or outside, at a time of day that is comfortable for you. Be seated with your back straight.
Level:	Intermediate/Advanced
Affirmation:	I am a positive person.

Steps:

1. Breathe, relax, and close your eyes. Enter the alpha state.

2. Make the choice that you want to have a positive mind-set.

3. Recall some times in your life when you felt really positive. Maybe it was graduating from high school, winning a contest, getting into college, or being hired for your first real job. Choose one of those moments and remember everything about it and how you felt. Feel the positivity in your body.

4. Now see yourself embracing the energy of positivity. Know that you are still that same person and can feel the same again. See yourself feeling the positive energy and taking it in. Again, feel it in your body as well as your mind.

5. If there is an activity or person that puts you in a negative place, see that place or person and watch them get smaller and smaller in your mind's eye. The result will be that they will have less of a negative effect on you.

POSITIVITY EXERCISE 23
LETTING GO OF STRESS

Stress, in all its many forms, is what holds us back the most. Reducing stress frees your mind so that you can create, problem-solve, and just feel good about life. You can use the practice to alleviate stress and to keep it from building by doing mini-visualizations (60 seconds) where you see your stress floating out of you. This visualization will allow you to think more clearly and stay focused.

Time:	5–15 minutes
Place:	Indoors or outside, at a time of day that is comfortable for you. Be seated with your back straight.
Level:	Intermediate/Advanced
Affirmation:	I am letting go of my stresses.

Steps:

1. Breathe, relax, and close your eyes. Enter the alpha state.

2. Scan your body and see the places where you are holding stress (most likely your chest, back, or stomach). Notice how that part of your body feels.

3. Once you have identified where you hold stress, take a deep breath and start to visualize that part of your body relaxing and the stress getting lighter and lighter. See it fading away and feel the relaxation in your body. (If you are feeling tense throughout your body, you can do a progressive muscle relaxation.)

4. Think of what may be triggering your stress. Is it a problem at work? At home? Once you find a trigger of stress, visualize it as something that you can overcome and then brush off. Imagine it is just a feather lying on your shoulder.

5. Now look at how you hold on to stress. For example, do you hold your breath when you are stressed? Do you get anxious or angry, feeling a tightness in your shoulders? Visualize yourself holding on to stress and then letting go of it. See yourself replacing your stress with a feeling of lightness and positivity. As the feather floats away, your body feels lighter and free of stress.

POSITIVITY EXERCISE 24
FOCUS ON THE GOOD

Most people believe good things just happen, and sometimes they do. But there is much more positive energy and good available to you than you probably realize. And you can bring it in with some simple visualization combined with relaxed deep breathing. Getting rid of bad vibes and feelings can be as easy as an exhale, and bringing in the good is only a deep breath away. Every exhale releases the negative and every inhale takes in the positive. By using your breath as a focus, you will stay more centered, and it will be easier to find and feel the good that is within and around you. Many people have psychological blocks to feeling good. Guilt, PTSD, anxiety, and depression are just a few of the things that block us. The good news is that you can overcome the blocks by training your brain, and that effort will yield a positive habit that will make your life better.

Time:	10–15 minutes
Place:	Indoors or outside, at a time of day that is comfortable for you. Be seated with your back straight, or you can do this while walking.
Level:	Intermediate/Advanced
Affirmation:	I am bringing more good into my life with every breath.

Steps:

1. Take a deep breath and continue breathing slowly and deeply throughout the entire exercise. Allow your mind to relax as well. If seated, you may want to close your eyes. Focus on entering the alpha state.

2. As you continue to breathe, with each inhale, visualize that you are taking in the good: Imagine yourself breathing in good energy, good ideas, and good health, or anything that you want more of in your life.

3. Take another deep breath, in and out.

4. Now on each exhale, see the "not good" leaving your body and mind, and allow yourself to feel your body lightening. As you breathe deeply, you may notice yourself relaxing and also feeling more energy.

5. Just keep breathing, in and out, bringing in the good and releasing the bad.

POSITIVITY EXERCISE 25
THE POSITIVE HEART

If you take a little time to look at your feelings, you may
find that most of the negative ones are in your head, even
if your heart is broken. Heart energy is pure, free from self-
judgment and doubt. The heart only wants to feel positive,
and negative energy stops you cold. By using the power of
visualization, you can lower your blood pressure, increase
positivity, and rid yourself of negative thinking. If this works
for you only 1 percent of the time, it's worth the effort.

Time:	10–15 minutes
Place:	Indoors or outside, at a time of day that is comfortable for you. Be seated with your back straight, or you can do this while walking.
Level:	Advanced
Affirmation:	My heart is light and feeling positive.

Steps:

1. Breathe, relax, and begin by entering the alpha state.

2. If your eyes are open, see and take in the good around you, like the people who love you, your environment, and your favorite hobby. If your eyes are closed, visualize the good within you, like your kindness, talents, and intelligence. (You can switch the order of where you focus each time you do the exercise.)

3. When you see or visualize something good, also see that goodness entering your brain and body through your mind's eye. Feel its warmth, like you are sitting in front of a roaring fire in a cabin with loving friends. Now bring it into your heart as well. Feel the goodness throughout your psyche.

4. As you take in the good and let it fill you, notice that the good feeling is all you feel. There is no room for bad. Know that this can be a practice that you can do anytime and anywhere. Remember that.

CHAPTER 3

RELATIONSHIPS

cannot overstate the importance of relationships. Every interaction we have with another human being is a relationship, and our primary relationships help us define our lives, set our goals, and bring us the most happiness and fulfillment. Our connections with those closest to us motivate us to get out of bed in the morning and succeed at work and in life. They are our greatest concern. Adding visualization to your relationship tool kit will make the difficult relationship moments easier and also help you create more joy. And who doesn't want that?

Case Study

The first love of my life passed away more than 30 years ago after a battle with cancer, and I truly did not think I could fall in love with anyone ever again. I could not even consider the possibility of love, because if I lost it again, I would just die.

It was a decision made out of pain. Loneliness set in rather quickly, and I allowed myself to sink into a deep depression that took over without me realizing it. I didn't know then that loneliness and isolation are very hard on our brains and bodies—and that living this way can be quite toxic. At that time all I knew was that what I was doing was not working for me and I needed to do something different.

I had begun working with Dr. David Bresler at the UCLA Pain Control Clinic. It's a world-famous program and advocates for a lot of visualization. It seemed only natural to use this powerful psychological practice, and so I began creating mindful, guided visualizations for myself.

At first the practice was about healing my broken heart, but after a number of months and some recovery, I was able to start seeing myself being in another relationship and feeling happy again. I continued the practice for a very long time, and I dated and waited for the right person to appear. Eventually she did. I was able to tell because our first conversation was four hours long and the rest were equally as deep. I felt like she "got me," and we were married 18 months later.

Visualization can help you find the right relationship, improve your communication, help you and those around you, and create a nicer life.

Not a day goes by without some kind of visualization and affirmation practice in my marriage. It's a part of us now because we know how effective it is. I would no sooner stop using (and teaching) visualization than I would stop eating. I need it to live and to be happy.

Guidelines on Cultivating Relationships

Positivity is one of the most important and endearing qualities a person can have. If you seek a partner, do yourself a favor and find a positive person. Kindness is also of primary importance: You want someone to be nice to you (and you to them).

When looking for a life partner, remember you are in it for the long term. Looks fade, fast cars get old, and sex tends to slow down after a few years. The qualities you need to find are the ones that will last.

Use the following visualizations to bring more love into your life and to help you have the kind of loving relationship that others just dream about.

RELATIONSHIPS
EXERCISE 1
ATTRACTING THE
PERFECT PARTNER

Attracting the right person into your life can be a challenging adventure. It's interesting to note that often what might initially attract you (looks, means, personality) is not what keeps you in or makes for a great long-term relationship. What you need most is mutual emotional support. When you know that someone has your back and is willing to be there for you in as many ways as possible, that person is a perfect partner.

Time:	10–15 minutes
Place:	Comfortably seated, indoors or out
Level:	Beginner
Affirmation:	I am attracting the perfect person into my life.

Steps:

1. Find a comfortable position. You can be seated or lying down, indoors or out.

2. Begin with your relaxation breathing, and enter the alpha state. Then imagine what it would feel like to be loved by the perfect partner.

3. Picture in your mind's eye the form of a person, not a specific person but just a rough outline of a figure, and hold it there for a couple of minutes. Imagine that this person whom you've never met is right for you. This person has all the qualities you want in a partner. Repeat those qualities to yourself, and feel what it is like to be in the presence of someone who is right for you.

4. Now see yourself next to the yet-to-be-met person and see that form putting their hand on your heart. As that happens, allow yourself to experience what that might feel like. That same feeling may be very close to what you feel when you meet the one who is perfect for you.

5. Repeat the affirmation silently to yourself as you continue to visualize the perfect person coming into your life.

RELATIONSHIPS
EXERCISE 2
HUGGING VISUALIZATION

Hugs are so powerful, but it's important that they come from the right person. I need a specific hug in the morning. I want to feel my wife's hand on my heart as we hold each other. Mind you, that can make for some interesting positioning in the early morning hours, but it's so worth it. When hugs come with love, they are very rewarding. You can't be concerned with anything but the outcome. Making great hugs happen is one of the tools that will make your relationship thrive.

Time:	10–15 minutes
Place:	Anywhere with your partner that is comfortable for both of you
Level:	Beginner
Affirmation:	Hugs are an important part of my life.

Steps:

1. Stand, sit, or lie down with your partner. State to one another that the goal of this visualization is to feel closer to each other.

2. Begin with your relaxation breathing, but this time do it together, with the same rhythm and timing. Inhale together and exhale together. Enter the alpha state.

3. Now hug each other, and visualize your embrace as a healing and uplifting energy force that is making both of you feel better and is making your bond stronger. Visualizing this together will make it happen. Know that.

4. Use this visualization to create anything you want as a couple. You can see yourselves getting a new car or planting a garden together and loving it. You can simply see yourselves together and not fighting with each other.

5. Talk about the goals of this visualization before and after each time you do it to refine the process and make sure you are getting what you need.

RELATIONSHIPS
EXERCISE 3
HEALING HEARTACHE

We all have emotional wounds that can subconsciously drive us and our behavior in ways not conducive to a good relationship. In other words, when we hold on to hurt, it can make us act like jerks. However, the love of a positive relationship can heal your own emotional wounds. Your heart gets nurtured (and nursed) back to wholeness when you let in the love of another person. When the two of you take time to focus your energies on one another, each partner gets a significant dose of unconditional love, which is an uncommon thing in adult relationships. This has a healing and bonding effect on the two of you.

Time:	10–15 minutes
Place:	Anywhere with your partner that is comfortable for both of you
Level:	Beginner
Affirmation:	Our love heals my heart.

Steps:

1. Stand, sit, or lie down with your partner. State to one another that the goal of this visualization is to heal some emotional pain in one of you: One partner will be the healer and the other partner will be healed.

2. Begin with your relaxation breathing, but this time do it together, with the same rhythm and timing. Inhale together and exhale together.

3. Feel the love you have for each other as you are right now. Then, if you are the partner who is the healer, begin to concentrate your energy on the person who is receiving this healing visualization. Look at and feel the energy in your partner's heart.

4. Now visualize your energy healing your partner's heart. For example, imagine your love is in the shape of a glowing heart and see it overlapping your partner's heart and thereby strengthening it. As you do this, the emotional bond between you also gets stronger. Allow yourself to feel that as well.

5. Now switch places and let your partner give you some emotional healing, because we all need it.

RELATIONSHIPS EXERCISE 4
UP-LEVELING COMMUNICATION

Communication is the most important thing in any relationship, and it is also perhaps the most neglected. People who communicate easily, honestly, and with kindness simply have the best relationships. It doesn't matter if you are in love, talking with your parents or siblings, or having discussions with coworkers—if you don't come from a good place, you will weaken that relationship. The objective of communication should be to share information, make decisions, and enjoy it, and doing one or all three is perfectly fine. If you go in without an agenda, it will make this process much easier. It is always best to communicate from a neutral emotional and psychological place, and this visualization will help you prepare for any important communication.

Time:	10–15 minutes
Place:	Seated in a comfortable chair
Level:	Beginner
Affirmation:	I communicate freely and clearly, and my true desires are spoken.

Steps:

1. Begin with your relaxation breathing. Focus on entering the alpha state.

2. Pick someone in your life with whom you are having some difficulty communicating. Picture that person sitting across from you also doing a visualization of their own.

3. See the two of you communicating nonverbally and see the other person understanding you and responding in a respectful manner. Keep this picture of the flowing communication in your mind's eye for several minutes.

4. As you complete the exercise, see and hear the other person saying to you that they understand what it is you are communicating with them and, lastly, see them saying "Thank you."

RELATIONSHIPS EXERCISE 5
A COUPLES COMMUNICATION EXERCISE

Good communication with the person you love is one of the best things on earth. Bad communication is one of the worst. Keeping your communication positive is not just luck; it takes some work and practice. By visualizing supportive and open conversations with your partner, you are taking a big step to ensure that the vast majority of your interactions will be positive. This will happen because you are establishing a good pattern as well as a plan for how you will deal with emotional triggers if they arise. Once your communication is pure, you will never question your partner's intent or desire.

Time:	10–15 minutes
Place:	Seated in a comfortable chair
Level:	Beginner
Affirmation:	The communication I have with my life partner is amazing.

Steps:

1. Begin with your relaxation breathing. Enter the alpha state.

2. Picture you and your life partner having a deep conversation and see it going very well.

3. As the conversation continues in your mind's eye, feel your own emotions and where you might get triggered. Think of your trigger: It might be harsh criticism or words that you take as criticism.

4. See yourself recognizing the trigger but not reacting to it. Just notice the trigger (the criticism) like you're looking at it from a distance. You do not have to react. This takes some practice.

5. The next step of this process is to visualize yourself talking with your partner about your trigger in a calm way. Also see your partner taking in your emotions and saying the words you would like to hear.

RELATIONSHIPS EXERCISE 6
RESPOND, DON'T REACT

Typically, when someone says something we don't like, we have a negative reaction. If that person is close to us, our reaction could hurt their feelings, and you never want to do that to someone you care about. Making the choice to respond reasonably to what someone has said, rather than react in an emotional way, is really the way adults need to communicate. Even if your relationship is only casual or work-related, choosing how to respond is going to get you so much more of what you want and need. You will also expend far less emotional energy and enhance your cognitive abilities—and people will just like you more. This visualization will help you learn to respond rather than react in communi-cation. You can also use it before you go into a conversation that you are concerned about.

Time:	10–15 minutes
Place:	Seated in a comfortable chair
Level:	Beginner
Affirmation:	I choose to respond and not to react to communications.

Steps:

1. This visualization is best done seated in a comfortable chair. Begin with your relaxation breathing and focus on entering the alpha state.

2. Visualize a communication in your life where your reaction threw the conversation out of balance. It could be a recent conversation with your partner or with anyone you know.

3. Once you have the conversation firmly planted in your mind, ask yourself, at what point could you have responded differently? Visualize the moment when the conversation derailed. What could you have done differently in that moment to make this communication better?

4. Imagine the conversation going differently, better. Imagine a resolution.

RELATIONSHIPS EXERCISE 7
ENHANCING EMPATHY

Empathy means having the ability to feel what another person is feeling. It is an important part of any close personal relationship, and while it sounds simple enough, it can be very emotionally taxing. Visualization can help strengthen your emotional forces so that you become more comfortable with the feeling. It can even help you with people in your life who could use a little more empathy. If you are a highly sensitive person, you are probably already too empathic, and you can use visualization to make yourself more tolerant to the feelings that you are taking in.

Time:	10–15 minutes
Place:	Seated in a comfortable chair
Level:	Beginner/Intermediate
Affirmation:	I feel comfortable being empathetic.

Steps:

1. Begin with your relaxation breathing. Enter the alpha state.

2. See a person in your life toward whom you need to be more empathic (alternatively, see someone you wish felt more empathy toward you).

3. Visualize yourself seated across from that person, and allow the feeling of empathy to flow between you. Staying with the basic feeling or sense of empathy will enhance the experience of giving and receiving empathy.

4. Once you have a good grasp of the empathy you need or want, you can use this same exercise to focus on a specific issue you want to resolve or emotion you want to be understood.

5. Allow this exercise to fortify you as you go out into the world, giving and receiving empathy.

RELATIONSHIPS EXERCISE 8
TENDERNESS

Tenderness is love given gently. With all the stress of dealing with daily life, your relationship needs to be a refuge from the world. When tenderness is part of that connection, it makes things on all levels easier. Knowing that you can find honesty and direction without harshness will help your relationship and your love grow. Opening yourself up to being more tender with your loved ones gives you more depth, understanding, and comfort in your relationships. This visualization will help you express tenderness together.

Time:	10–15 minutes
Place:	Anywhere with your partner that is comfortable for both of you, seated or lying down, or facing each other and touching in some way
Level:	Beginner/Intermediate
Affirmation:	Tenderness is a part of our relationship.

Steps:

1. Begin with relaxation breathing, and breathe together as a couple. Look into each other's eyes. Hold hands.

2. See the feeling and action of tenderness. It might be a white light or a velvet blanket, whatever image you like. See this tenderness enveloping and caressing you. Allow yourselves to feel this tenderness as you look at each other.

3. If tears start to come, just let them. Be in the moment. If unhappy moments from the past interrupt your thoughts, just acknowledge them and know that this process with make them fade away.

4. Keep your focus on the energy of tenderness between the two of you.

RELATIONSHIPS EXERCISE 9
AVOIDING ARGUMENTS

All arguments are a choice. If you want your life to be nicer and your relationships to be better, give up arguing, and disagree calmly instead. Once you make the mental decision that you want to give up arguing and reinforce that decision with visualization, you are well on your way to eliminating 90 percent of what you once thought was worth arguing about. This visualization is best done with your partner, though you can adapt it to do on your own.

Time:	10–15 minutes
Place:	Seated in comfortable chairs as a couple
Level:	Beginner/Intermediate
Affirmation:	I do not have to engage in arguments, especially with the ones I love.

Steps:

1. Begin with your couple's relaxation breathing (where you inhale and exhale at the same time). You can also keep your eyes open and look at each other as you visualize. It may help to hold hands.

2. As you visualize, look deeply into the eyes of the one you love. Remember an argument that left you both feeling pretty bad (and you can have different memories). Don't spend a long time here, just get a quick picture.

3. Now look into your own heart and see how you could have avoided hurting the one you love. You may have some pain about your part in the argument, and that will let you see how you could have done things differently. Remember that.

4. Take 100 percent responsibility for the argument. It is a solid cognitive psychological tool to keep it from happening again. As you feel and visualize all of this, remember your partner is having their own journey.

5. At the end, share your experiences. It will only make you closer.

RELATIONSHIPS EXERCISE 10
RECEIVING LOVE

For many people, it is more difficult to let love in than to give it to someone. You can go into psychoanalysis to find out why, or you can accept that, up until now, receiving love was hard for you. This visualization will help you change that. Receiving love from another person is what makes us whole. Many people have blocks to this because they also lack the necessary self-love that makes one feel worthy of getting love from someone else. The truth is that letting in another person's love can help you find the love for yourself. It's an internal win-win. This is a great exercise for emotional healing and growth. It can also be adapted to do with your partner.

Time:	10–15 minutes
Place:	Anywhere that is comfortable for you
Level:	Beginner/Intermediate
Affirmation:	I feel comfortable allowing love into my life and heart.

Steps:

1. Begin with your relaxation breathing. Focus on entering the alpha state.

2. If there is someone close to you who you know loves you and yet you have a hard time feeling it, picture that person and wrap them in a warm loving light.

3. Now focus on their heart and see the love that is there come out and wrap itself around you like a warm light. As it does, allow yourself to feel the warmth that comes with it. Feeling it physically as well as emotionally will help imprint the process.

4. As you allow the love to enter your psyche, it may bring up past memories that were painful. Just be mindful that these memories are being pushed out to allow you more room to feel what's positive.

5. Embrace the newfound feelings of loving and being loved.

RELATIONSHIPS
EXERCISE 11
FOCUS ON WHAT'S RIGHT

Much of the time we look at our relationships from a "what's wrong" perspective. We sometimes only see flaws and foibles in the person we are bonded to and in those around us. This is something that visualization can help us reverse. This is an exercise you will want to repeat a number of times to change the habit. And when you see someone you love doing something right, tell them. This visualization can be done on your own or with your partner.

Time:	10–15 minutes
Place:	Anywhere that is comfortable for you
Level:	Beginner/Intermediate
Affirmation:	I see those around me doing the right things.

Steps:

1. Begin with your relaxation breathing and enter the alpha state.

2. Visualize a mental picture of the person you love. Now see yourself in a moment when you were being hard on them and see (and feel) how they feel when you are like this. Stay there for five minutes.

3. Notice any emotional sadness that you may feel, but don't dwell on it. You may feel some guilt that comes with the realization that you have been hard on someone you love. It's natural to feel this way, but it serves as a reminder that you want to behave differently.

4. Again, just notice any feelings of sorrow or guilt. Refocus your sorrow on the person you have hurt. Imagine how they must feel. Now take a deep breath, and imagine apologizing to this person, seeing them taking in your apology, accepting it.

5. After this exercise, you can have a conversation about changing this behavior with the other person. It is a very healing thing to do.

RELATIONSHIPS EXERCISE 12
FRIENDLY FAMILY GATHERINGS

Have you let your in-laws become outlaws? Do you dread getting together with family members on the holidays? Are there family members who you feel don't like you? All of these issues can be quelled with the practice of visualization. Although you are only one component in the mix, visualizing that your family has no real control over you will make interacting easier and can remove a great deal of the tension in the room. If you project an aura of peace and understanding, it's pretty hard for other people to want to cast negativity at you. You can get to that state by protecting your psyche with this practice. Knowing that you are not at fault and that you do have some ability to change these situations is very empowering. It helps calm things down, not just for you but for those you love as well. You can also adapt this visualization to do with your partner or as part of a family group.

Time:	10–15 minutes
Place:	Seated in a comfortable chair
Level:	Beginner/Intermediate
Affirmation:	My family is loving, and I do not let them throw me off balance.

Steps:

1. Begin with your relaxation breathing. Enter the alpha state.

2. Visualize your family being at peace with one another. Picture everyone at the table laughing together or in the living room quietly talking or playing board games—whatever comes to mind. Take your time. This may take a little while to get used to.

3. Once you have a picture of everyone together, allow them (one by one) to express themselves in a way that triggers an issue for you or for someone else. You can recall a past event, if it helps. When this happens, now see the person stopping to realize that they made a mistake. They said the wrong thing or did something that they now regret doing. Watch them apologize. See it a few times for each person.

4. Also see yourself not getting triggered. If someone is acting in an inappropriate way, you grow calmer. This mental exercise keeps you relaxed in the face of being annoyed (or worse). Allow the feeling of calm to wash over you, so that your body feels relaxed and calm. Take in that you have this ability.

RELATIONSHIPS EXERCISE 13
OUR LOVELY LIFE

For most of us, life is busy, and sometimes we can forget our lives are really good. Not feeling good about your life can lead to anxiety and depression, and it can make it very difficult to focus on what is important. If you've had a temporary setback, allowing yourself to see the good things in your life is a great tool for creating emotional balance. In this visualization, you are going to cement the fact that you have a good (or great) life to share with those you love. Remember, it's not about how many toys you have or how many followers you have on social media. A good life is about being comfortable and having the love you desire around you. This visualization can be done on your own, or adapted to do with your partner, or as a group or family exercise.

Time:	10–15 minutes
Place:	Seated in a comfortable chair
Level:	Beginner/Intermediate
Affirmation:	We have a lovely life.

Steps:

1. Begin with your relaxation breathing. Enter the alpha state.

2. Visualize the good parts of your life and your relationships. It's fine to go from one thought to another in this exercise. List them in your mind, like counting your blessings.

3. Pick out the best parts and put an imaginary star next to them. Each time you do this, feel the joy that comes from having a lovely life, and take in the emotion.

4. If there are parts of your life that you want to improve or change, picture them in your mind, and then take the feelings you have from the star experiences and layer these over the things you need to fix. The joy that you receive from acknowledging all that is good in your life actually empowers you to improve your life in other areas.

5. As you combine the feelings of the best parts with the things you want to accomplish, imagine them getting resolved and the feeling of balance and harmony that enters your life.

RELATIONSHIPS EXERCISE 14
OUR COMPASSIONATE CONNECTION

Compassion—a combination of empathy, concern, kindness, and consideration—is essential for most close relationships, especially the one you have with your partner. By demonstrating your compassion, you are making it known that you are not just there for your partner but also really care about what they are going through. Compassion is also good for your love life. When someone understands that they are cared for in this manner, they will be more open to a passionate relationship, too.

Time:	10–15 minutes
Place:	Seated in a comfortable chair
Level:	Intermediate
Affirmation:	Compassion is a part of my life and love.

Steps:

1. Begin with your relaxation breathing. Enter the alpha state.

2. Visualize your partner or someone you love, and see that person's compassion flowing from them like an imaginary waterfall. Allow the compassion to flow over to you and through you. Allow it to physically and emotionally envelop you.

3. Now imagine yourself being compassionate. You can imagine a moment with your partner or with someone else. See yourself listening to others calmly and kindly. Notice their response. See how the dynamic changes when you are compassionate. Notice how you feel in your body.

4. If you are in need of more compassion, you can visualize it coming to you from the same people that you share yours with. Stay with the visualization until you feel the compassion physically.

RELATIONSHIPS
EXERCISE 15
CREATING DEEPER INTIMACY

Physical intimacy is one of the most important parts of a relationship, but it should never be the primary concern. Having a deeply intimate relationship involves very profound, life-changing emotions. Sharing the intimate parts of yourself can be scary, but that can be softened with visualization. When you open up to another person on a deep level, be prepared for your own feelings to change and grow in a positive way. Intimacy makes us cherish life more. You can do this visualization alone or with your partner.

Time:	10–15 minutes
Place:	Seated in a comfortable chair or lying in bed with your partner
Level:	Intermediate
Affirmation:	My love relationship is deeply intimate.

Steps:

1. Begin with your relaxation breathing. Enter the alpha state.

2. Visualize your partner and think about what intimacy, both physical and nonphysical, means to you. Think about how it appears in your love life and in your communication.

3. If you are doing this with your partner, open your eyes and look at each other, allow yourselves to feel the love between you, and visualize where you can increase your intimate connection. See what it is you would like to be doing with your partner, and it's okay to fantasize. Visualize the two of you connecting in this way. (You can talk about this after the exercise.)

4. When you find a place in your intimate connection that needs some healing or just a minor tune-up, bring that issue to the center of your visualization and see it getting the healing and refining that you seek. As you see this happening in your mind's eye, also feel it in your body. If you are with your partner, end this process with a long, slow hug.

RELATIONSHIPS EXERCISE 16
HEALING MY PARTNER

In every relationship, at some point, one or both of you will have a health concern. You can help each other using visualization, which has a profound healing ability. Giving someone healing energy is rooted in ancient healing traditions that predate modern medical science, and it works. This visualization is best done with your partner.

Time:	10–15 minutes
Place:	Indoors, best done at bedtime and upon awakening. You can be seated, but lying in bed is also good.
Level:	Intermediate
Affirmation:	My partner is being healed and getting better.

Steps:

1. Begin with synchronized relaxation breathing.

2. Hold your partner and place your hand(s) on the part of their body that is ailing. You can also just give them a full-body hug.

3. As you touch your loved one, visualize a healing energy coming from you and entering their body and being. You can picture this as a white light or a beam of energy. Now visualize the disease lifting away from your partner's body, drifting away, leaving your partner lighter and healed.

4. Feel your hands getting warm as the healing happens. You may also be able to feel a physical sensation between your hands and your partner's body. Keep the connection as long as it is comfortable, and hold on to the visualization of your partner getting well.

RELATIONSHIPS EXERCISE 17
RELEASING CONTROL

We can all feel controlled by our loved ones, and sometimes we want to control them. We all like to get our way, but when you truly love someone, you want them to have their way as much as possible. But control is actually an illusion. By releasing it in your relationship, you are allowing your love to flow more freely and reducing the opportunity for useless conflict. Relationships are not about control but about an emotional, psychological, and physical balance. This visualization will help get you there. It's best to do this visualization with your partner, but you can adapt it to do on your own.

Time:	10–15 minutes
Place:	Indoors, at a time of day that is comfortable for you. Be seated with your back straight.
Level:	Intermediate
Affirmation:	We are a balanced and loving couple. There is no need for control in our relationship.

Steps:

1. Hold hands with your partner. Breathe, relax, and begin.

2. If your eyes are open, look into each other's eyes deeply. Imagine your love as a river flowing between you, joining you. Visualize how your love creates this strong bond between the two of you that you both feel and honor. Sit with the feelings that this brings up.

3. Now recall a moment when you thought you needed to exert some control over your partner. You wanted something that you couldn't get. Notice how you felt then. Maybe you were tense, angry, or stressed. Notice what you did in that moment. No need to judge, but just notice what you wanted in that moment and believed you couldn't get unless your partner changed in some way.

4. Now release that feeling of control or need for control. Relax and sit with the feeling of release.

5. Feel the dedication you have to one another. Letting go of control, allow your love to flow freely.

RELATIONSHIPS
EXERCISE 18
COMFORTABLE WITH COMPROMISE

Somewhere in a thesaurus far, far away, there is another word for marriage—"compromise." What may be one of the most important parts of a relationship has gotten left out of the wedding vows. Compromise gives couples direction in how to take a relationship from the battlefield to blissful coexistence. Compromise is not a hard lesson, once you realize the gifts that come from it. Learning to work together will make your relationship and your life a better place to be. Visualizing yourselves coming to a compromise in most every situation is a way to psychologically prepare yourself. You can do a version of this visualization alone, but it is best done with your partner. Learn to set compromise as your default communication method, and you will live happily ever after.

Time:	10–15 minutes
Place:	Indoors, at a time of day that is comfortable for you, seated or maybe lying down with your partner
Level:	Intermediate
Affirmation:	It is easy for me to compromise with my partner.

Steps:

1. Hold hands with your partner. Breathe, relax, and begin.

2. Look deeply into each other's eyes. Take in how your love creates a strong connection between the two of you, and enjoy that feeling of connection. (All couples should do this part every day.)

3. Recall a recent time when you reached a compromise together, and remember all the positives about that conversation. Also remember your mood, how you were feeling physically and emotionally. Were your mind and heart open to your partner?

4. As you remember that moment, feel the positive energy. Visualize yourselves repeating this same positive process over and over, each time you need to reach a decision together.

RELATIONSHIPS
EXERCISE 19
VALIDATION

Without enough validation from your partner, you will walk around every day feeling insecure. Withholding validation is a sign that there are deeper issues at play, but it may also just be that you never created the positive relational habit of validating one another. Think of giving and receiving validation as enhancing your emotional support structure: The more you feel validated and supported, the easier it is for you to deal with the twists and turns on the road of life. Without it, your psyche is vulnerable to anxiety, depression, and constant questions about the safety of your relationship. Some people find it easier to give validation than to receive it. This visualization will help you open your mind and emotions to both giving and getting this valuable relational component.

Time:	10–15 minutes
Place:	Indoors, at a time of day that is comfortable for you. Be seated with your back straight.
Level:	Intermediate
Affirmation:	It is easy for me to give and receive validation.

Steps:

1. Hold hands with your partner. Breathe, relax, and begin.

2. Look deeply into each other's eyes. Visualize the validation that you want to give your partner. It can be anything you want, like an imaginary validated golden ticket. Whatever comes to mind is just fine. It's part of the process.

3. As you see the validation in your mind's eye, watch yourself presenting this validation to your partner, thanking your partner and giving them a hug.

4. Now imagine your partner bringing validation to you.

5. Now feel the warm glow of being validated, and let it move through your entire being and body.

6. Keep your focus on the physical and emotional sensations, and on your ability to both give and receive validation.

RELATIONSHIPS EXERCISE 20
UP-LEVEL OUR LOVE LIFE

Most couples have sexual dry spells or experience a time when one person needs intimacy more than the other. Visualization is the perfect tool to help prevent or overcome these temporary glitches in your physical relationship. It is important to remember that blame and pressure do not work. You just need to come from a place of true love for each other. This pure love energy has a profound psychological effect on both of you. It will help build the "cuddle hormone" oxytocin, which will make both of you feel more affectionate.

Time:	15–60 minutes
Place:	Indoors, at a time of day that is comfortable for you. Best in bed.
Level:	Intermediate/Advanced
Affirmation:	Our love life is perfectly balanced.

Steps:

1. Relax and hold each other closely.

2. Feel the love you have for your partner and allow that feeling to wash over you. You can visualize the love you have for your partner as a ribbon of light and energy that connects the two of you. Allow yourself to feel that energy. Then feel (or give your partner) a powerful embrace. Take in this feeling and image and feel the love at the same time.

3. Now see your love mixing with your partner's love until the energy between you merges. As your partner does the same, feel the charge of your psychic connection and romantic bond.

4. Feel this connection for the rest of your time together, and then talk about what you experienced to cement it into your consciousness.

RELATIONSHIPS
EXERCISE 21
TOGETHERNESS VISUALIZATION

The reason you got into a relationship in the first place is that you really, really loved this person and wanted to spend your life with them. But between work and life, you may not get to spend as much time together as you would like. Fortunately, visualization can help you see and create new opportunities to be with, and closer to, the one you love. This visualization is best done with your partner, but you can adapt it to do on your own.

Time:	10–15 minutes
Place:	Indoors, at a time of day that is comfortable for you. Be seated with your back straight.
Level:	Intermediate
Affirmation:	My love and I spend a lot of quality time together.

Steps:

1. Hold hands with your partner. Breathe, relax, and begin.

2. Look deeply into each other's eyes. Then close your eyes. Visualize being together in ways that you have not yet been able to. Perhaps you are spending your entire day together, working together or traveling together.

3. Experience what togetherness feels like to you and what it feels like to your partner. Once you know the experience of togetherness by feeling it, a committed couple can feel connected no matter what.

4. Now feel the warm glow of being in a loving relationship, and let it move through your entire being and body.

5. Keep your focus on the physical sensation and on your togetherness.

RELATIONSHIPS
EXERCISE 22
FROM DISCORD TO HARMONY

We all get ticked off at our loved ones and friends—it's normal. The problem is that most of us spend too much time walking around with negative energy racing through our bodies until the issue is resolved. Instead of letting the feelings fester, you can work on your own emotional regulation. This will help you deal with the situation from a calm and balanced perspective.

Time:	10–15 minutes
Place:	Indoors or outside, at a time of day that is comfortable for you. Be seated with your back straight.
Level:	Advanced
Affirmation:	I take responsibility for my own emotions.

Steps:

1. Breathe, relax, close your eyes, and enter the alpha state.

2. Find the place in your body where the negative energy is focused—a place that is hurting—and put your hands there. You can also just wrap your arms around yourself in a light embrace. This will fortify you and intensify the visualization process.

3. Focus on the upsetting thing you are dealing with, but as if you were standing at some distance away, looking at yourself. From this perspective, imagine how you could have handled the situation better. What would you have said or done differently?

4. Imagine the other person listening and being understanding of where you are coming from.

5. Now review what the other person said, and concentrate on understanding what the other person is really trying to say to you.

6. Visualize the conversation resolving and feel the good feeling that comes with it. Repeat this until you have the confidence to have the talk for real.

RELATIONSHIPS
EXERCISE 23
PARTNERSHIP PARTICIPATION

Sometimes we leave the relationship up to our partner and just go with the flow. That can be okay, but the person you are with may want a break from carrying all the relational energy. If you don't think you come up with good ideas for making your relationship better and better, it's time to change that mind-set and join in on the fun. Besides, your other half needs and desires your participation because relationships are a team sport. This exercise can be done solo or adapted to do with your partner.

Time:	10–15 minutes
Place:	Indoors or outside, at a time of day that is comfortable for you. Be seated with your back straight.
Level:	Advanced
Affirmation:	I have a balanced and fun relationship with my partner.

Steps:

1. Breathe, relax, close your eyes, and enter the alpha state.

2. Visualize where in your relationship you would like more input and energy from your partner. This has to come lovingly from you; if you are upset, stop and begin again.

3. Imagine asking your partner for their input and your partner responding to your efforts or your needs.

4. Now imagine your partner asking you to give more to the relationship, and imagine yourself responding positively to your partner's requests.

5. If any past resentments come up, just notice them for a moment. Then imagine them on a cloud floating away.

6. Imagine a scene in which the two of you are doing something together. Maybe it's cooking a meal—because when two hearts and four hands are making a meal, it's not just food for the body but food for the soul—or anything that you would enjoy doing with your partner. Imagine the two of you responding gently and positively to each other. Allow the positive energy of this image to enter your heart. That's where growth first takes place.

RELATIONSHIPS
EXERCISE 24
GIVING MY ALL

Holding back your emotional energy from your partner can make the difference between a fulfilled relationship and one in which you are constantly looking for reasons and ways to leave. If you find yourself distracted from your partner and perhaps looking at other people online or on the street, it's time to redirect your emotions to where they belong. If you don't nurture the emotional side of your relationship, your psyche will start to give up and look around. This is a solo visualization but can be adapted to do together.

Time:	10–15 minutes
Place:	Indoors or outside, at a time of day that is comfortable for you. Be seated with your back straight.
Level:	Advanced
Affirmation:	I give my partner all my relationship energy.

Steps:

1. Breathe, relax, close your eyes, and enter the alpha state.

2. Visualize where you are right now in terms of feeling emotionally bonded with your partner. How close or far away are you from your partner? Is there a gap, and if so, how big is it? You have the power to close it.

3. Concentrate on your positive feelings for your partner. Recall what you love about them. You can recall a wonderful moment between the two of you, maybe the moment you met. Allow yourself to take in the positive feelings of that moment.

4. Imagine the gap between the two of you shrinking, as you are filled with love for your partner.

5. Now think of something that you can do for your partner to express your love, like giving a small gift. Imagine yourself giving this gift to your partner, and your partner returning the love with a smile or an embrace.

6. Spend the rest of the visualization just feeling what it is like to be whole and complete in your relationship. It will change how you direct your emotional energy.

RELATIONSHIPS EXERCISE 25
HONESTY

Most of us tell little lies every day—so convenient when you don't want to go somewhere, do something, or be with someone. But if used in your relationship, lies will erode the trust you have built together. When honesty is missing, the rest of your relationship puzzle cannot fit together. It all starts with honesty, and it's much easier to be honest and open than to try to hide anything. The truth is you should feel comfortable enough to have nothing to hide, which this visualization will help you see.

Time:	10–15 minutes
Place:	Indoors or outside, at a time of day that is comfortable for you. Be seated with your back straight.
Level:	Advanced
Affirmation:	I am open and honest in my relationship.

Steps:

1. Breathe, relax, close your eyes, and enter the alpha state.

2. Take a look at the times when you have not been honest with your partner. You may want to just focus on a recent moment when you were not honest.

3. Now look at what that lack of honesty has taken away from your overall dynamic. You can visualize what this dishonesty looks like. It may not be that big, but find it and give it a shape. Maybe it's a blotch of ink on a whiteboard.

4. Once you have this image in your mind's eye, see yourself erasing it—wiping it away, so the whiteboard is clean again. Pause and promise yourself that with this gesture, you are removing your habit of not being open and honest with your partner.

5. Take a deep breath. You may express a sigh of relief. It feels good to come clean. Allow that liberating feeling to wash over you. Repeat the process a few times.

CHAPTER 4

GOALS

We all need goals to focus our energy. When our goals are confusing and hard to pinpoint, our energy will be the same way. And that makes life much more difficult.

Setting and achieving goals is a psychological process, and visualization is one of the most important steps. But the first step is to decide where to focus your attention and to make sure that it's your desire and not someone else's. The mental imprinting works best when you are 100% emotionally invested.

Case Study

Walt Disney famously said, "If you can dream it, you can do it." He started his career with two things: his dream and his talent. A World War I veteran, Disney saw a world that needed entertainment and laughter, so he decided to get creative and do something about it.

Disney is perhaps the most beloved of the multitalented producer moguls—at once a writer, director, and animator—who ever lived. His work and brand are synonymous with family, fame, and fortune. So, it was a source of great intrigue when, in 1954, he decided to buy 160 acres of orange and walnut orchards in Orange County. What would soon be Disneyland was a secret to everyone but Disney and a select few, which made it more interesting to most everyone (and it kept the land cost down).

His goal was to create a place where families could enjoy his fantasy-come-to-life rides and attractions. Yes, he had a team, but the vast majority of the creations all came from Disney's vision. So did the growth of his company and the prosperity for those who continue to follow Disney's goals for a family-friendly entertainment environment. These days, Walt Disney's family values are still maintained as meticulously as the grounds of Disneyland itself.

However, Disney endured many setbacks and challenges in pursuit of his goal. Not everyone believed in his vision, and a lack of funding forced him to convince the American Broadcast Company (ABC) to invest in Disneyland's construction in exchange for some prime-time programming. His dream, his desire, and his determination kept him going through it all, and he prevailed because his dream helped him stay inspired, focused, and positive. Forty years later, the Walt Disney Company was so successful it purchased the very same ABC network, a testimony to the partnership forged by Walt Disney's ambitious goals.

Guidelines for Setting Goals

Creating goals and achieving them depends largely on how much energy you put into the process. Goals are not a set-and-forget process—they have to be nurtured. As you begin to establish goals, it's important to make sure that they are your own—not something you are trying to achieve because your parents or your boss told you to. Also make sure that your goals are realistic—not based in some alternative reality.

As you visualize your goal, always imagine it in positive terms: This is how you want your life to be. Next, figure out the steps needed to get there, and if you have a timeline, make it part of the goal. If you want to achieve something within a certain time frame, you need to plan starting backward from your deadline to make it happen.

And don't try to do everything at once!

To reinforce your goals, write them down and read them aloud to yourself or with your partner or team every day. This gives the goals more power, and you will reach them sooner. It also helps to discuss your goals regularly with others who may be involved.

As Walt said, "The way to get started is to quit talking and begin doing." So let's begin.

GOALS EXERCISE 1
CREATING MY SUCCESS

When you want to achieve something, it helps to visualize how success will feel. Visualizing success will reinforce your desire and confidence. The feelings we project attract the success we seek and also prepare us to deal with it. Knowing that you have succeeded at one thing in your life is all you need to help you reach your next goal. By visualizing that moment, you'll recapture the positive energy in your mind and body, and that energy will act as a launching pad for you to reach your latest dreams.

Time:	10–15 minutes
Place:	Indoors or outside, at a time of day that is comfortable for you. Seated or lying down.
Level:	Beginner
Affirmation:	I am successful at what I choose to put my energy into.

Steps:

1. Breathe. Relax your body and mind. Enter the alpha state.

2. Recall a time when you felt successful. It can be winning an athletic event or an election, getting your diploma, receiving an award, getting a raise or a promotion, or any circumstance that left you feeling that sweet smell of success. Picture the circumstances, your surroundings, and who was there to celebrate with you. Use all of your senses to re-create that moment and how you felt.

3. Bring that emotion into your consciousness and allow it to move through your body, so you can really feel it in the present. Relive the experience in your mind and body.

4. Now picture yourself achieving your current goal, and blend that feeling of past success with your current goal. Allow yourself to feel that successful feeling. As you watch and feel yourself succeed at your goal, notice that you now believe you will reach it. Keep that feeling going for the rest of your visualization.

GOALS EXERCISE 2
GETTING IT ORGANIZED

Too many papers on a messy desk and countless unread emails in your inbox get in the way of productivity. Sometimes a house entryway looks more like a counter at a car dealership than a humble home. A little visualization can motivate you to get your space and yourself more organized. If you do one thing every day, and do not make the clutter worse, it will get better. And you will feel better about yourself. Using visualization will help you make organization into a habit instead of a chore.

Time:	10–15 minutes
Place:	Indoors or outside, at a time of day that is comfortable for you
Level:	Beginner
Affirmation:	I am an organized and structured person when I want to be.

Steps:

1. Find a comfortable position, seated with your back straight. For this exercise, if you want to organize a room, being in that room will be helpful.

2. Begin with your relaxation breathing, and enter the alpha state. Close your eyes, and imagine yourself in organized and comfortable surroundings.

3. Experience the joy of being more organized, to imprint the feeling in your mind. Bring the feeling of being organized into your body and allow it to move through you, calming and relaxing your further.

4. Now imagine the room that you want to clean. (If you are in the room, you can open your eyes for a moment and look around.) Notice one area that you want to organize.

5. Now imagine it getting organized at hyperspeed, like in a movie scene. See all of your papers getting filed, your stacks being unstacked, and your workspace getting clear and clean. You may want to see yourself doing it with a supportive friend, real or imaginary.

GOALS EXERCISE 3
PROSPERITY

Most people want financial success, but very few ever attain financial independence. Perhaps you feel like you don't deserve it on some level, or that it will be too hard to make it in the current financial climate. But you are only limited by your goals, dreams, and desires. Visualization will help by removing unconscious roadblocks to your personal financial independence. I do this visualization on a regular basis because it always works.

Time:	10–15 minutes
Place:	Indoors or outside, at a time of day that is comfortable for you. Be seated with your back straight.
Level:	Beginner
Affirmation:	I am a financially independent person.

Steps:

1. Breathe, relax, and get into the alpha state. Close your eyes and begin.

2. See yourself in your current circumstance in life. Look at what you are doing, and see how money comes to you. Recognize all the hard work you do to earn your way, and feel good about yourself. Give yourself an imaginary pat on the back.

3. Now visualize a giant cornucopia, bigger than a house. Next, see money flowing out of the horn of plenty into your lap. It helps to have a specific amount that you'd like to get from a particular activity, project, or job—and keep it realistic. See what that will look like, and feel how it will affect you emotionally.

4. You can stack the money up and count it as it continues to flow to you. This exercise goes directly into your subconscious and will help you ask for what you need to gain financial independence.

GOALS EXERCISE 4
REPLACING MY DREAMS

Happiness comes from working toward what you desire, so once you have achieved a goal, it is very important to replace it with another. This visualization exercise does a number of positive things to your psyche. It allows you to continue to be happy, it helps you create new goals, and it helps you attain balance and peace of mind.

Time:	10–15 minutes
Place:	Indoors or outside, at a time of day that is comfortable for you. Be seated with your back straight.
Level:	Beginner to advanced
Affirmation:	I always have a dream I am moving toward.

Steps:

1. Breathe, relax, and get into the alpha state. Begin.

2. Visualize the last goal you achieved and how working toward that goal made you feel. Maybe it was finding your dream office. Remember when you were looking for the right spot, the excitement of looking and finally finding it, the view from the window over the water, the furniture you chose, the decorations.

3. Now visualize yourself after you reached your goal. Notice the initial feeling of contentment, and notice the feeling leaving you, so that you feel a little empty. There's no need to dwell on the feeling of emptiness, but do notice it. Now in that empty space, fill it with a picture of having a new goal. You don't need to visualize your goal yet, but visualize yourself busily working toward something positive in your life, and the positive emotions you feel when you are engaged in reaching a goal.

4. Finally, allow some possible new goals in. Initially, allow these possible goals to enter your mind as pictures that come and go of things you might want to do next in your life: They may be places you have never been but have always thought of visiting, a project in the garden, an addition on your house, a picture you want to paint. Do this process several times over a week, and the image that you see the most will be your next goal.

GOALS EXERCISE 5
PERSONAL POWER

Having personal power means having the ability to create, set, and achieve your goals. People who have it are admired, and those who do not constantly seek it out. The truth is that it can only be found in one place—within you. Visualization can help you get in touch with your personal power so that you feel it and acknowledge it to yourself. You own your power. This will help you reach goals that most people only dream about.

Time:	10–15 minutes
Place:	Indoors or outside, at a time of day that is comfortable for you. Be seated with your back straight.
Level:	Beginner to advanced
Affirmation:	I am internally powerful and have the ability to reach my goals.

Steps:

1. Breathe, relax, and get into the alpha state. Begin.

2. Visualize how you perceive your own personal power—what are your greatest strengths? You may need to step back to get perspective, so you can really see and appreciate your strengths like someone else would upon meeting you.

3. Now ask yourself where you could increase your strength or just change how you have been using it. For example, you might be a great cook who has always made wonderful meals for your family. Maybe you want to take that strength and do something different with it—maybe you want to open a restaurant!

4. Once you know what you want, visualize yourself getting it. You can concentrate on images, or you can concentrate on the feelings that accompany the thought of getting what you want. The point is to get your brain and body used to taking in and working with more personal power, allowing yourself to feel "I can do this."

5. Allow yourself to feel and experience your own personal power. Experiment with it in your visualization, and let your mind go where it wants to. You will see new ideas and directions if you stay with it for a while.

GOALS EXERCISE 6
STRENGTHEN MY BRAIN

It has been said that knowledge is power, and your brain is the source of that power. The better you can think, the more likely you will be able to realize your goals. Knowing that you have a high-functioning cognitive system in your head is very empowering.

Time:	10–15 minutes
Place:	Indoors or outside
Level:	Beginner/Intermediate
Affirmation:	I have a highly functioning brain.

Steps:

1. Get comfortable, and begin with your relaxation breathing to enter the alpha state. As you relax, gently put your hands on your head.

2. Visualize your brain in any form that pleases you. Maybe you imagine it as the latest supercomputer. You can see it working and making decisions, creating plans as well as helping you stay emotionally balanced.

3. Notice how it makes you feel emotionally and physically to see your brain working so efficiently. Keeping that picture in your mind's eye and feeling the power of your brain, you can begin to problem solve. Start with whatever is vexing you at the moment and notice how a solution comes to mind.

4. Once you have used this technique in visualization, you can use it again in immediate situations. Just think about the process and casually let the ideas flow in.

GOALS EXERCISE 7
I HAVE PERFECT HEALTH

We all know that without health, achieving success does not matter. The goal of near perfect health is attainable for most of us, and it can be made stronger through the process of visualization. If you are having some medical issues at the moment, use this exercise to see yourself healing faster. If you are feeling fine right now, use this exercise to maintain your good health.

Time:	10–15 minutes
Place:	Indoors or outside
Level:	Beginner/Intermediate
Affirmation:	I have perfect health.

Steps:

1. Breathe, relax, and get into the alpha state. Then begin.

2. Visualize your body and put a focus on any parts that are unhealthy. You may want to find a point of discomfort some-where in your body. This is the point where you will focus your healing thoughts.

3. Visualize healing that place in your body that is unwell. You may want to imagine a white light over the area. Breathe deeply and release the pain. Feel the discomfort lift and float away. If you have a difficult health condition or are battling any physical problem, this visualization will help you feel better faster.

4. If you are already healthy, use this time to feel the glow of radiant health, and visualize yourself maintaining this physical condition and accomplishing your goals.

GOALS EXERCISE 8
MY GOALS ARE WITHIN MY REACH

It's important to keep your goals realistic: You may never be six-foot-four or coordinated enough for the NBA. Your subconscious will naturally rebel against you visualizing any goal that is out of your reach. You will have trouble relaxing and focusing on the goal. So be sure to set practical goals. It's also important to recognize that no goal has ever been reached in one try. It may look that way, but all success takes preparation, and visualization is one of your best tools. By visualizing success, you are allowing your brain to rehearse and get prepared for achieving your goals.

Time:	10–15 minutes
Place:	Indoors or outside
Level:	Beginning/Intermediate
Affirmation:	I am achieving my goals.

Steps:

1. Breathe, relax, and get into the alpha state. Begin.

2. Pick one of your practical goals and visualize yourself approaching it. Perhaps in your mind's eye you are walking toward your goal. As you get nearer to your goal, are there any roadblocks? If you see any, imagine thrusting them aside with just a wave of your hand as you continue to walk toward your goals.

3. If you feel stress as you approach your goal, again, simply wave it away with your hand. Reaching your goals is as gentle and easy as walking down the road. Visualizing this will make getting there a lot more fun.

4. See yourself reaching the goal and feel good about it. Let these positive feelings wash over you.

GOALS EXERCISE 9
MY TIMING IS PERFECT

The phrase "perfect timing" invokes images of rare opportunities, like when the sun is shining after the rain has stopped so that a rainbow appears. Now just imagine that you have the ability within you to time things perfectly—for yourself. If your goals do not suit this time in your life, perhaps they are best put on hold until you are ready to pursue them. Timing can be everything, and if you make the proper preparation, and you plan well, you can achieve anything.

Time:	10–15 minutes
Place:	Indoors or outside
Level:	Beginning/Intermediate
Affirmation:	I have perfect timing.

Steps:

1. Breathe, relax, and get into the alpha state. Begin.

2. Imagine a wonderful working clock within you that helps you keep perfect time.

3. Get a visual picture of the clock (it can be analog, digital, or even a sundial), and watch the clock keeping time. Sit with this image for a while. Breathe in and out, peacefully watching time move forward.

4. Now come up with a practical goal where timing is important. For example, you could imagine yourself having enough money in the bank for a down payment by the end of the year. Now, see yourself moving forward at the perfect pace to reach that goal.

5. As you visualize achieving your goal, feel your own pride rush through your brain and body. Doing the visualization can help you meet deadlines by imprinting the importance of timing on your sub-conscious. This way, you won't feel rushed or pushed.

6. You may also add steps where you pause to check on your progress along the path or where it would be appropriate to take a break to recharge your energy.

GOALS EXERCISE 10
MILESTONE VISUALIZATION

Big goals, like climbing the tallest mountain, take more time. It's best to break larger goals into bite-sized chunks or milestones. Three to five milestones along the way are most effective. It's best to acknowledge and celebrate after you reach each milestone, reviewing what you've already accomplished, and then set your sights on the next one.

Time:	10–15 minutes
Place:	Indoors or outside
Level:	Intermediate
Affirmation:	I easily reach my milestone goals.

Steps:

1. Breathe, relax, and get into the alpha state. Begin.

2. Visualize the goal you want to reach and get a very strong picture of it in your mind's eye. For example, you might be imagining changing jobs or even changing careers, buying real estate, or forming a new company. Make sure that you get more detailed each time you picture it.

3. Next, as you visualize the goal, ask yourself if you can see natural steps along the way toward the process of reaching it, and allow those images to come to you visually. You can also listen to your thoughts here. As an example, what would you need to do to change careers? Would you need to take classes or work at something for a while for less pay? Would you need to save up money before you could buy a house or start that company?

4. Now arrange these steps in their natural order and see how they are each a separate goal and a milestone along the way to reaching your ultimate goal.

5. Picture your first small goal or milestone. Remind yourself that small goals are relatively easy to attain. As you picture yourself reaching this goal, see yourself celebrating with friends, acknowledging your success. Then see yourself moving forward to the next goal.

GOALS EXERCISE 11
SERVICE GOALS

If you are a giving person, creating goals that help others will be a part of your practice. When your goal serves the greater good, you gather strength from all those who participate in the same thing and from those in need. This creates a great deal of empowerment. And with that kind of power, you can reach any goal.

Time:	10–15 minutes
Place:	Indoors or outside
Level:	Intermediate
Affirmation:	My personal goals also serve others.

Steps:

1. Breathe, relax, and get into the alpha state. Begin.

2. In your mind's eye, imagine how your goal will serve others. It could be volunteering at a local homeless shelter, rescuing or fostering animals, mentoring parentless teens, or anything that feels right to you. See yourself doing this service, and begin with that image in mind.

3. Imagine helping just one person reach their goal or just helping them do a little better in life. Visualize this person. What do they look like? What do they say? Helping others feels good. Take that feeling inside and experience it with all your senses.

4. Visualize the smiles on the many faces of those you have assisted with your goal, and see that your goals have a wider reach than you would have ever expected. Experience that emotion, too.

5. Are you ready to reach out for your goal of helping others? It's a win-win. Figure out the steps you need to take, and go for it.

GOALS EXERCISE 12
WRITTEN GOALS

When you write down your goals, you have a much better chance of reaching them. When you write something down, it becomes at least twice as powerful in your mind. Written goals also serve as reminders of what you are reaching for and what you have accomplished so far. With this in mind, a goal achievement worksheet can help you visually track where you are going and also to see your milestones. On this sheet, you list your goals, the steps, and the timing, along with who will support you and how you are feeling. Reviewing the worksheet reinforces your progress. This next visualization will inspire you to use a worksheet to accomplish your goals. (If you'd like a copy of my goal achievement worksheet, go to my website at BartonGoldsmith.com and put the word GOALS in the message box of the contact form.)

Time:	10–15 minutes
Place:	Indoors or outside
Level:	Intermediate
Affirmation:	When my goals are written, I achieve them faster and am more productive.

Steps:

1. Breathe, relax, and get into the alpha state. Begin.

2. Visualize yourself creating or working on a goal achievement work-sheet. Imagine what your worksheet would look like, the columns and the headings, with short-term goals listed and milestones along the way toward bigger goals. What else would you like to add to the worksheet?

3. Visualize yourself writing down a goal and, just like that, you complete the goal! Each time you write down a goal, it is completed right before your eyes.

4. As you reach bigger milestones, see yourself checking them off on your worksheet as you move ever closer to your desires. Feel the progress in your brain and body.

5. After you have completed a big goal, you can give yourself a big A++. See it, feel it, and bring it into reality.

GOALS EXERCISE 13
CREATING A
WONDERFUL FUTURE

No one knows what the future will hold, but visualization can give you a lot more confidence in where you are headed and what the outcomes will be. By visualizing a wonderful future, you are setting yourself up to have one. You can use this visualization to work on current goals or to create new ones.

Time:	10–15 minutes
Place:	Indoors or outside
Level:	Intermediate
Affirmation:	I see a wonderful future ahead of me.

Steps:

1. Breathe, relax, and get into the alpha state. Begin.

2. See what a wonderful future will look like. Visualize a beautiful home and family, a great job or business. Allow yourself to dream a little. Those dreams are visions of your goals, and you can reach them. If you have some specific goals that you've already been working on, you can also imagine reaching them.

3. Once you have an image of your future in mind, believe in it with all of your psyche. Know that just by imagining it, you are helping make it happen.

4. Breathe deeply and gently smile to yourself. Take in the positive feelings in your mind and body. Feeling the wonderfulness of it all is important. Allow yourself to feel good about your future.

GOALS EXERCISE 14
THINGS I WANT

There is nothing wrong with wanting things, as long as your possessions don't possess you. Visualization can help you make those dreams a reality. This is an all-in visualization, meaning that using all of your senses will make it work better. This exercise is inspired by one of the first "prosperity preachers," Reverend Ike, who said, "You can go to the ocean with a teaspoon or a bucket. The ocean doesn't care." You can do this visualization solo or with others.

Time:	10–15 minutes
Place:	Indoors or outside
Level:	Intermediate
Affirmation:	I will accomplish my big dreams.

Steps:

1. Breathe, relax, and get into the alpha state. Begin.

2. Visualize yourself sitting in the car of your dreams. (Note: It will help if you have already seen it, touched it, and taken it for a test drive.) Now use all your senses.

3. Start by hearing the purr of the engine, and then turn up the radio. Next roll down the windows and feel the breeze in your hair. Then feel the steering wheel in your hands, and finally smell that new car smell.

4. Visualize yourself driving down the road with your loved ones all enjoying your new ride and the accomplishment of getting it. All of your senses are working together to strengthen the image and imprint it on your psyche so that getting what you dream of having will just be a natural part of your life.

GOALS EXERCISE 15
LONGER LIFE

Years ago, while conducting a visualization workshop, I received word that my father was dying. He was in Las Vegas, and I was in Los Angeles, and I took the first flight out. When I arrived at the hospital, he was still alive but in pain. I held his hand and visualized him getting well. (Meanwhile, back in LA, one of my interns was leading the class in a group visualization of my father getting through the night and healing.) The next morning, my father was awake and alert, and the doctors were confounded. He actually lived for another few months, and I got to spend a lot more time with him. It was an incredible gift that I will never forget.

Time:	10–15 minutes
Place:	Indoors or outside
Level:	Intermediate
Affirmation:	My visualization is helping this person heal.

Steps:

1. Breathe, relax, and get into the alpha state. Begin.

2. Visualize the person you wish to help heal.

3. Send this person healing energy from your heart and head. You can picture this as a white light, a beam of energy that can reach someone even if they are far away. Putting your hand on your heart can help magnify this projection.

4. Visualize the person getting better. See them getting up and walking around. See them smiling and feeling good.

5. If you can, visit in person and do this with them.

GOALS EXERCISE 16
CHOOSING THE RIGHT PATH

We all have to make choices in our lives. By using visualization, you allow your psyche to take in all the positive and negative feelings and possible outcomes of different choices. The answers to all of our questions are within our subconscious. We just need to take the time to look.

Time:	10–15 minutes
Place:	Indoors or outside
Level:	Intermediate
Affirmation:	I am on the right path.

Steps:

1. Breathe, relax, and get into the alpha state. Begin.

2. Visualize the decision you are struggling with and look at all sides of it. Your decision may involve other people and emotional, physical, or financial commitments. Consider which of these aspects of the decision are a source of struggle and how that struggle makes you feel.

3. Now start to alter the vision. What if you were to give up this goal or change your mind? Notice what that alternative reality looks like and how you would feel. Is this vision freeing? Is it disappointing? If any issues come to you as you consider this new vision, ask yourself out loud, "Is there anything I need to know?" Asking this question can help you explore your choices.

4. Lastly, explore alternatives that may come to mind. Just allow your mind to explore what would happen and how you would feel if you decided to do something else. Allow your feelings to guide you as to how to move forward.

GOALS EXERCISE 17
MINDFULNESS VISUALIZATION

Mindfulness has become very popular in recent years, although the practice has been around almost as long as visualization. Mindfulness is a form of meditation in which you concentrate on being in the present moment, noticing everything in that moment without judging anything. By practicing visualization, you are practicing a form of mindfulness. Mindfulness can also keep you in emotional balance as you deal with your visualizations becoming actualized. Some people would say that you have to separate the two exercises, but I believe that visualizing yourself being mindful in the world will only make this ability stronger and easier to access. You can do this visualization solo or as part of a group.

Time:	10–15 minutes
Place:	Indoors or outside
Level:	Intermediate/Advanced
Affirmation:	I am a mindful person.

Steps:

1. Breathe, relax, and get into the alpha state. Close your eyes and begin.

2. Visualize yourself in a place of calmness and serenity. It can be real or imagined, such as floating on a cloud or being in a huge library (like in *Game of Thrones*) where you can find any answer, or just sitting by a river and listening to the rushing water.

3. From this place, release any tension or fears you may have within you. Focus on the present moment. You can do this by simply paying attention to your breathing, in and out, in and out. If thoughts of the future or the past come up, gently notice them and allow them to go. Bring your mind back to your breath in the present moment. If you start to worry about some aspect of your life, or about a goal that you have, observe the worry as a passing thought like any other. Watch it come and go.

4. Stay relaxed and calm, and as other thoughts enter, continue to refocus on the present moment, as you breathe in and out. If ideas for reaching your goals come to mind during this meditation, they will be there for you to return to later. The goal of this exercise is to experience and deepen your mindfulness and sense of calm, which will make achieving your goal a natural process.

GOALS EXERCISE 18
ENJOYING THE PROCESS

If you understand that education is a process but graduation is an event, then you have the ability to be patient with yourself as you strive toward your goals. It can feel like it is taking forever, but you will get so much more accomplished if you flow with the process instead of chasing after the end result. Enjoying the process is a great way to deal with life, generally, and certainly makes coping easier when things don't go exactly according to plan. You can do this visualization solo or as part of a group.

Time:	10–15 minutes
Place:	Indoors or outside
Level:	Intermediate/Advanced
Affirmation:	I am enjoying the process of this adventure.

Steps:

1. Breathe, relax, and get into the alpha state. Begin.

2. Visualize your current life adventure, the process that you are most focused on right now: It could be one or more of many things, like receiving training or education, building a business, or looking to get married.

3. Emotionally take in that you are in a process of enriching yourself, and notice how your body feels when you think about what you're doing and all that you are achieving. You may also be excited about the future. It's normal to notice this. Just remind yourself that the future is less important to your well-being than what you are doing right now. Seek this balance and see how it makes you feel inside.

4. Now visualize yourself achieving your goal, starring in the event, and feeling great about the process. This will make it easier for you to take on the next project and the next great adventure.

GOALS EXERCISE 19
DOING WHAT I WANT

Most people go to school or get trained to do a job they simply tolerate because they falsely believe that they cannot do what it is they really love. Visualization is a tool that can help you do what you love for a living, or at least have enough joy to make the rest of your life work. If you want to make a change and follow your heart, then creating an action plan in your mind is the first step. Making this happen may take some time, so be patient with yourself and the process. It is also important to keep this visualization realistic: You are probably not going to win the lottery. This visualization can be done solo or as part of a group.

Time:	10–15 minutes
Place:	Indoors or outside
Level:	Intermediate/Advanced
Affirmation:	I am doing what I love for a living.

Steps:

1. Breathe, relax, and get into the alpha state. Begin.

2. Visualize your dream career, but keep it realistic. If you want to be a star on Broadway, then use that goal as long as you have the skills. Be honest.

3. See yourself opening doors, and each door represents a different opportunity. Maybe it's an offer to play the lead in a community theater production. Maybe it's a dead end. Each door leads you to possible steps toward living your dream gig (which is how it works in real life). You may have to go through quite a few doors before you see something that catches your eye, and when you do, then stop and enter. That is your next step.

4. Visualize yourself taking this step. After you have done it in real time, repeat this visualization to see the next step. Do this until you get where you want to go.

GOALS EXERCISE 20
CREATING A FAMILY/TEAM

Most everyone wants to be on a team or part of a family with people who share the same goals. For a team, obviously, there are many personalities to contend with, so the best way to approach getting on that team (or landing a job with a company) is to make yourself desirable to the other members. The same thing holds true for finding a partner and creating a family. The most wonderful part about it is that both situations will bring out the best in you. This visualization can be done solo or as part of a group.

Time:	10–15 minutes
Place:	Indoors or outside
Level:	Advanced
Affirmation:	I love the people I live and work with.

Steps:

1. Breathe, relax, and get into the alpha state. Begin.

2. Visualize your current family or workplace team. (You can also visualize the family you would like to have someday or your ideal working team, if you're not part of one now.) See things flowing and going the way you would like, for example, where you would like to be and who would be with you.

3. Visualize the best relationships and results coming from your connections with others. If it helps, recall how you solved a recent issue together. Concentrate on the feeling of successfully resolving the issue with others in your life.

4. Recognize how you are balancing work and family in good ways. Doing this visualization with others will strengthen your bond and make it easier to resolve future issues when they arise.

GOALS EXERCISE 21
CONTRIBUTING TO SOCIETY

Knowing that you contribute to your community gives you a feeling that you are a valuable human being who is changing the lives of those you are assisting. If you don't know where to start, a quick Google search will show you many local charities to choose from. If you are ambitious, start your own.

Time:	10–15 minutes
Place:	Indoors or outside
Level:	Advanced
Affirmation:	The service I lend to my community returns to me.

Steps:

1. Breathe, relax, and get into the alpha state. Begin.

2. Picture the kind of service work you would love to do. Be open to ideas coming to you. For example, it could be working with children, helping the elderly, building a park or a community center, or supporting a cause you believe in.

3. Once you have your focus, watch yourself making changes in your community, offering your help to others who could use it. You can also imagine how those small changes may impact the whole planet. Get a sense of the value that you bring to those you serve.

4. See yourself having helped dozens of people over the years. Now imagine the smiling faces of those whose lives you have touched looking at you and saying "Thank you." Now take that in.

GOALS EXERCISE 22
TRAVELING THE WORLD

Much has been said about the value of new experiences over material things. Both are important. (Personally, I want to travel the world *and* have a nice home to come back to.) Most people have difficulty making even one of these goals happen because they do not give either enough focus.
This next visualization will focus on the goal of traveling the world. Of course, there's no guarantee that visualizing yourself climbing the Matterhorn is going to get you there, but it's a start. You can do this visualization solo or with your partner.

Time:	10–15 minutes
Place:	Indoors or outside
Level:	Advanced
Affirmation:	I get to travel the world.

Steps:

1. Breathe, relax, and get into the alpha state. Begin.

2. In your mind's eye, picture the place you would most like to visit. It is best to start with one destination in mind, so that your focus is more intense.

3. Picture the place, the people, and the activities that you would like to engage in while you are there. Visualize, taste, and smell the great food, the lovely place you are staying, and feel the joy of just being there throughout your body.

4. Also visualize that you will have the time and the money to take this trip. If you need to save up, see that process being easy as well. Even visualize getting through airport security with no problem.

5. Visualize every detail, no matter how small. Visualizing it will help make it happen.

GOALS EXERCISE 23
DREAM HOME VISUALIZATION

Having a comfortable home environment helps you feel good about life, but creating it can be complicated. Money is perhaps the biggest issue, but you can make any house a home with the right attitude and enough love. Making your dream home is about more than just visualizing, but this process can also lead you to the answers and assistance you need. Put those in your visualization as well. And the more people you can get to see the picture with you, the stronger the result will be.

Time:	10–15 minutes
Place:	Indoors or outside
Level:	Advanced
Affirmation:	There's no place like home, and mine is perfect.

Steps:

1. Breathe, relax, and get into the alpha state. Begin.

2. Visualize the home of your dreams, but keep it realistic—remember, someone already lives in Buckingham Palace. What does it look like on the outside?

3. When you get a picture of your ideal place, go inside and look around. What's special about this home? What makes it feel so much like home? Is it the kitchen? What's there? Light filtering through the window onto clean countertops? The view of the lake beyond? What do you love most about this home? Take in your surroundings and enjoy the feeling of being in your dream home.

4. You may already be living in your almost-dream home and just want to improve it. Visualize what it is that you would like to do.

5. Visualize the process, including finances, going smoothly, as you make your dream home come true. Visualize a gathering of family and friends in your home.

GOALS EXERCISE 24
A JOB WELL DONE

Finding your perfect career can be a challenge. And some-times something else comes along, and you just have to go for it. "Right livelihood," as it is sometimes called, is really one the best things in life. Having a job that you love to do every day is quite a nice way to make a living—some would say it's the only way. Visualization has brought me everything I have—from radio and television shows to columns, blogs, and books. The very same and more can happen for you. You can do this visualization solo or as part of group.

Time:	10–15 minutes
Place:	Indoors or outside
Level:	Advanced
Affirmation:	I love the work I am allowed to do.

Steps:

1. Breathe, relax, and get into the alpha state. Begin.

2. Visualize yourself loving what it is you already do, even if you don't really love it right now. Concentrate on the best aspects of your job. Making friends with your current gig will help you get to the next.

3. Visualize where it is you would like to go and what you would like to do. It might be a job related to what you do now, or it could be something completely different. Allow your imagination to wander.

4. When you get a picture of your ideal job, see yourself doing it. Then in your mind, backtrack to see how you got there. Did you just need to make some phone calls? Did you have to go back to school to gain more expertise? Imagine the steps to realizing this goal. Then focus your attention on the first step.

5. Trust that what you are doing right now is a stepping stone to the next phase of your career path, and see just that next step. When you open your eyes, you will be ready to take it.

GOALS EXERCISE 25
A LIFE WELL LIVED

The affirmation for this final exercise may be a tiny bit Zen. It amplifies that the process of visualization is one that can help you lead a good life. Knowing that you have used your talents and abilities for the good is an empowering feeling that will enhance your current circumstances, so hold on to this knowledge and the feeling that it inspires in you. Know that you are a good person who has lived a good life and helped those you care for in times of need.

Time:	10–15 minutes
Place:	Indoors or outside
Level:	Advanced
Affirmation:	I am honored to live a good life.

Steps:

1. Breathe, relax, and get into the alpha state. Begin.

2. Visualize your whole life. You can imagine this as a movie like in *Boyhood* or *63 Up*, watching yourself grow up and develop into adulthood and beyond. Focus on all the good that you have done.

3. This is a time for positive thoughts. If a negative memory arises, just wave your hand and flick it out of your vision.

4. Take the good feelings from what you have given in your life and imprint them on your goals for a better future. That will cement them in your psyche.

Resources

Creative Visualization for Beginners, by Richard Webster

Creative Visualization: 6 Positive Days of Guided Visualization Techniques—Unlock Creative Thinking and Your Life Potential Through Meditation, by Mia Rose

Creative Visualization: Use the Power of Your Imagination to Create What You Want in Your Life, by Shakti Gawain

E-Squared: Nine Do-It-Yourself Energy Experiments That Prove Your Thoughts Create Your Reality, by Pam Grout

Positive Visualization: How It Makes Marvels Throughout Your Life: Know the Benefits of Visualization and Learn the Technique to Attain Life Goals, by Myrone Meyers

Practical Guide to Creative Visualization: Manifest Your Desires, by Melita Denning and Osborne Phillips

The Mental Movie Method: How to Use the Power of Visualization to Program Your Mind for Success, by Raza Imam and E. A. C. Andrews

The Power of Your Subconscious Mind, by Joseph Murphy

Turning Dreams into Reality: Change Your Mindset and Effortlessly Achieve Your Dreams, by Yuval Tabib

Visualization and Imagery: Harnessing the Power of the Mind's Eye, by Rav DovBer Pinson

References

Baars, B. J., and N. M. Gage. *Cognition, Brain, and Consciousness*. 2nd ed. Amsterdam: Elsevier, 2010.

Ellenberger, H. F. *The Discovery of the Unconscious: The History and Evolution of Dynamic Psychiatry*. New York: Basic Books, 1981.

Gawain, S. *Creative Visualization: Use the Power of Your Imagination to Create What You Want in Your Life*. 40th anniversary ed. Novato, CA: New World Library, 2016.

Haley, J. *Uncommon Therapy: The Psychiatric Techniques of Milton H. Erickson, M.D.* Reissued ed. New York: W. W. Norton and Company, 1993.

Ranganathan, V. K., V. Siemionow, J. Z. Liu, V. Sahgal, and G. H. Yue. "From Mental Power to Muscle Power—Gaining Strength by Using the Mind." *Neuropsychologia* 42, no. 7 (2004): 944–956.

Silva, J., and P. Miele. *The Silva Mind Control Method*. New York: Simon and Schuster, 1977.

Simonton, O. C., S. Matthews-Simonton, and J. L. Creighton. *Getting Well Again*. Reissued ed. New York: Bantam, 1992.

Skottnik, L., and D. E. J. Linden. "Mental Imagery and Brain Regulation—New Links Between Psychotherapy and Neuroscience." *Frontiers in Psychiatry* 10 (2019): 779.

Index

Acknowledgments

I would like to thank Callisto Media and my editors (in order of appearance): Katie Parr, Elizabeth Castoria, Shannon Criss, Mo Mozuch, and Brady Kahn.

I would also like to thank the publications and media that have supported my writing and work over the past several decades. I owe a big debt of gratitude to the editors of PsychologyToday.com and my 22 million readers. Thank you to Johnnie Miller-Cleaves of the *Chicago Tribune* and Tribune Media for your unwavering support.

I would also like to acknowledge Drs. David Bresler, Martin Rossman, Albert Ellis, Milton Erickson, Elizabeth Kubler-Ross, M. Scott Peck, David Viscott, Bernie Siegal, and Harville Hendrix for their support and their profound works and teachings in the field. I have learned so much from all of you.

To my loving wife and family, you are all that I live for. Thank you for always and in all ways supporting me in everything that I do.

And thanks also to Mr. Bob Dylan; your words and music are a visualization for our world.

Barton Goldsmith, PhD, an award-winning psychotherapist, writer, and speaker, has been a nationally syndicated columnist for more than 20 years. His columns have been published in more than 500 newspapers worldwide, and he has written more than 3,000 articles. He has been a psychotherapist for more than 30 years specializing in on-set therapy for the entertainment industry.

Since 2002, his weekly newspaper column, which is syndicated by Tribune News Service, has been featured in hundreds of publications, including the *Chicago Tribune* and the *New York Daily News*, among many others. He is also a top blogger for *Psychology Today*, and his blog, *Emotional Fitness*, has had more than 22 million views.

He has also authored several books, including *Emotional Fitness for Couples: 10 Minutes a Day to a Better Relationship*; *Emotional Fitness for Intimacy: Sweeten and Deepen Your Love in Just 10 Minutes a Day*; *Emotional Fitness at Work: 6 Strategic Steps to Success Using the Power of Emotion*; *100 Ways to Boost Your Self-Confidence: Believe in Yourself and Others Will Too*; *The Happy Couple*; and co-authored *100 Ways to Overcome Shyness*.

He is the creator of the visualization app MyCancerFighter. He continues to write, do media interviews, and work with clients from all over the world.

"Dr. G" began working in the field of psychology when his career in professional basketball was cut short because he only grew to five feet, six inches tall.

His website is DrBartonGoldsmith.com.

CPSIA information can be obtained
at www.ICGtesting.com
Printed in the USA
LVHW020736270320
651341LV00001B/1